J. Stephen (James Stephen) Jeans

Pioneers of the Cleveland Iron Trade

J. Stephen (James Stephen) Jeans

Pioneers of the Cleveland Iron Trade

ISBN/EAN: 9783744721974

Printed in Europe, USA, Canada, Australia, Japan

Cover: Foto ©Suzi / pixelio.de

More available books at **www.hansebooks.com**

PIONEERS

OF THE

CLEVELAND IRON TRADE,

BY

J. S. JEANS,

AUTHOR OF "WESTERN WORTHIES," Etc.

MIDDLESBROUGH-ON-TEES:

H. G. REID, "GAZETTE" PUBLISHING OFFICES,

1875.

PREFACE.

THE extraordinarily large and rapid growth of the Cleveland Iron Trade, and the vast population chiefly dependent upon it, has awakened an interest which extends beyond the district immediately concerned. The fact that the make of Cleveland Iron now amounts to 1,999,491 tons annually—being more than a third part of the whole make of England, and fully double the annual production of Scotland—invests it with a national importance. To supply some definite knowledge of the men who have created this great industry, is the purpose of this volume.

The following chapters originally appeared as a series of articles in the *Newcastle Weekly Chronicle,* and a strong desire was expressed by many to possess them in a more permanent and convenient shape. Before reproducing them in book-form, the facts were carefully verified, but it is obviously no easy matter to secure in the circumstances, perfect accuracy. The aim has been to give a full and faithful sketch of the men who have chiefly come to the front in the creation and development of the staple trade of Cleveland, without going outside the functions of the biographer and the historian.

No doubt, some names deserving of mention have been omitted; and opinions may differ as to the relative positions assigned to the various pioneers. The time has not yet come for doing justice to the newer works and workers;—the introduction of wire, nail, tube, and other manufactures, on which the future prosperity of the district must largely depend. No attempt at classification has been made, and it is hoped that the book will be accepted as an honest endeavour to preserve some reliable and tangible record of the inner life of the Cleveland district, and the lives of the men who have helped to raise it to the position which it now occupies.

CONTENTS.

I.—CHARLES ATTWOOD.

IT would be difficult to find, in the whole range of industrial biography, a more remarkable career than that which it is here our province to trace. Belonging to, and living chiefly in the memory of a past generation, Charles Attwood is less known, and still less understood and appreciated, than he deserves to be, by the children and children's children of those whom he has outlived. Many of the reminiscences here recorded will have seen the light of publication for the first time, and many facts that clear up what have hitherto been little else than vague traditions, will here, also, initiate their existence on paper. In tracing the lines of Mr. Attwood's biography, we are cultivating a field of surpassing promise and ripeness. Science owes him much—more, probably, than his successors will ever be willing to acknowledge. In the troubled arena of politics he has also fought and left his mark —a mark that it will be difficult to efface. His

B

many-sided and versatile character may be approached and estimated from several different points of view; but his career almost naturally divides itself into two parts—the scientific or industrial, and the political.. We prefer to deal first with the former phase, as more germane to the aim and scope of the present work.

Mr. Attwood belongs to a family that had long occupied a leading position among the ironmasters of South Staffordshire. His grandfather began the manufacture of iron in that county about the middle of the last century. At that time, the iron trade of Staffordshire was of extremely limited extent. Scrivener, in his work on the "Iron Trade," estimates the total quantity of pig iron made in England and Wales in 1740 at 17,350 tons, or less than the annual production of a single large-sized Cleveland blast furnace at the present day. In Staffordshire the staple of the pig iron was made up into nail rods and bars. It was in this branch of the trade that the Attwood family were chiefly engaged, although they had previously become steel manufacturers. on a scale that was considered at that time of day, to be exceptionally large. Indeed, the steel manufacture of Great Britain was then the monopoly of a few families. The grandfather of Mr. Attwood, with his three sons, took a leading place among the monopo-

lists. The bulk of the steel was made from
the iron obtained from the ore of Dannemora
in Sweden, called Oregrund iron. There were
four firms in Great Britain that monopolised
the Dannemora iron for steel-making purposes, and it may be interesting, at this time
of day, to state that these firms were the Attwood family—which included the father of
the subject of our sketch—the Walkers of
Rotherham, the Cooksons of Newcastle, and
the Harveys of Bristol. It was in this trade
that the Cookson family laid the foundations
of their fortune, and the Harveys also
amassed immense wealth in it, until in an
evil hour they founded the Ebbw Vale Works
in South Wales, where they lost much of what
they possessed. As for the Attwoods, they
continued to stick to the steel trade, which,
however, was becoming less of a monopoly
than it had previously been. The Sheffield
firms were getting possession of the field with
their cheaper steel, made from Russian and
from second class brands of Swedish iron;
and competition with them could only be
maintained by fighting them with their own
weapons and on equal terms. This the Attwoods hesitated to do, although young Charles,
who had been brought up to the steel trade,
and had studied it closely, thought that the
Dannemora ore could still be used with more
advantage. Full of this faith, he would have

liked to be allowed to carry on the works on
his own account. "Don't be such a fool,
Charles," said his relatives. " Can't you see
the trade is shrivelled up ? We haven't half
the trade we used to have. These Sheffield
people, with their cheap steel, are beating us
out of the field." " Which," said young Attwood, "they will continue to do, so long as
you charge cent. per cent. profit, while they
are content with five-and-twenty." Charles
persevered in his suit, assuring his father that
he saw how to make their works compete with
the Sheffield firms, but he could not get his
own way, and he had to look out for " fresh
fields and pastures new."

About the year 1810, we find Mr. Attwood
acquiring a share—no more than a tenth—in
a small window or crown glass manufactory at
Gateshead. In this concern he worked
vigorously, and was enabled in 1813, after
buying out all his partners, to carry it on
as his own exclusive property. Meanwhile,
he felt that the manufacture of glass was in
anything but a perfect state, and set himself
to improve it. He was so successful, that he
patented an invention enabling glass, instead of being in colour, as Mr. Attwood has
himself put it, "something like a goose's
egg," to assume the smooth and transparent
consistency it now retains. It was three years
before he was able to bring his process to

the degree of perfection he desired. During those years he worked most assiduously. He had an office in London, to which the greater part of his glass was shipped for sale ; and he had just attained the threshold of complete commercial success—the works having passed entirely into his own hands, and his new process being remunerative—when he became involved in one of the most disastrous lawsuits that ever disgraced the annals of the Court of Chancery,—and that is saying much. " It is," says Mr. Attwood himself, " a curious tale. One day I was sitting in my London office—it was in the autumn of 1813—when a strange man entered and asked if I was Mr. Attwood. Upon my replying in the affirmative, he handed me a note and a piece of parchment, which was a summons to appear in the Court of Chancery at the suit of 'Barber *versus* Banner.' I said, 'I never knew or heard of any such people in my life.' He said, 'Oh ! just put it into the hands of your solicitors, and you will see it's all right.' " Mr. Attwood followed his strange monitor's advice, and found that he had unwittingly become involved in a law-suit of long standing, and of almost interminable complication. The principals to the suit—Barber and Banner— had bought a small glass bottle work at Gateshead, which they ultimately converted into a manufactory of ground glass. Barber, who was a solicitor in Newcastle, was a speculative and unscrupulous man. He soon ruined his partner Banner, and, having been threatened with a prosecution for forgery, suddenly disappeared. Meanwhile, Banner was declared bankrupt, and his assignees, thinking, perhaps, there was little or nothing to be got, failed to realize the estate. The works, however, were carried on by other parties until they were joined by Mr. Attwood; and the bankrupt's representative, finding meanwhile that there was something in the business after all, brought a suit to recover the profits for upwards of 20 years, under a decree of the Court of Chancery, ordering an account between himself and the two original partners. The case stood in this position when Mr. Attwood became involved in its meshes. It was a question whether the case would not hold out until the account was rendered, and whether the works would not follow the title of the buyers. In the flush of prosperity, Mr. Attwood determined to fight out the case to the last. His first counsel was that Mr. Bell who took up a foremost position at the Chancery bar in the earlier half of the present century. But the case "dragged its weary length along," year after year, until Mr. Bell having become old, addressed Lord Eldon one day, and said, 'I am sorry to inform your lordship that I do not purpose to practise any longer in your

lordship's court." "Why," said his lordship,
"how's this—surely a precipitate decision?"
"Well, your Lordship, I'm an old man."
"So am I," said Eldon. "But," said Mr.
Bell, "I'm an infirm old man." "And so,
also, am I," said the Chancellor. "Well,"
said Mr. Bell, driven at last into a corner,
"the real fact is, that, I've made enough money
and wish to retire." "Aye," replied his
Lordship, " but you have the advantage of me
there." Mr. Bell having retired from the
management of his case, Mr. Attwood had to
look out for another leading counsel. He
procured the services of Mr. Peps, afterwards
Lord Chancellor of England, whose patience
also became exhausted before the suit was terminated. "We must get a hearing," he said
one day, addressing Mr. Attwood, "or this
case will last as long as your grandchildren."
At last, after twenty-eight parties involved in
the case had been gathered together from all
parts of the world—after nine years of cease-
less and costly litigation, and after exhausting
the time, means, and patience of more than
one party to the suit—it came before the
Court for final judgment. Vice-Chancellor
Leach, who has attained some notoriety, from
having been selected by George the Fourth to
prosecute Queen Caroline, declared, in dis-
missing it, that it was a most melancholy
case and a disgrace to the records of the

court. To Mr. Attwood it meant little short of absolute ruin. His patent, which should, and under other circumstances would have made him one of the richest men in the country, was only of fourteen years' duration. Three of those years had been spent in bringing it to perfection. Other nine had been frittered away in a vexatious and costly litigation, which completely unhinged his prospects, and created a gnawing sense of insecurity. When the trial terminated, he found that the parties from whom he should have recovered his costs were mere men of straw. He was thus the poorer by thousands of pounds. With only two years of his patent unexpired, he could not hope to do great things. So far, therefore, as he himself was concerned, he jogged along until his patent rights had lapsed, when Mr. Chance of Birmingham, Mr. Hartley of Sunderland, and other firms up and down the country took up the principle and worked it out with highly profitable results. Briefly stated, Mr. Attwood's patent consisted in the use of pure soda, pure lime, and pure sand, unmixed with the Scotch kelp and Spanish barilla that were formerly used exclusively in the manufacture of English window glass.

It is impossible to resist the temptation to relate another reminiscence of Mr. Attwood's connection with the glass trade, which led to an encounter between himself and Sir Robert Peel, who was then Secretary of State for Ireland. A statutory enactment having provided that a duty of 250 per cent. on its prime cost should be imposed on all glass entering Ireland, Mr. Attwood resolved to take advantage of the short intervening space, before the Act became law, to get as much stock as possible into the sister country free of duty. Simultaneously with this, the Dumbarton glass makers—then the largest in the kingdom—shipped immense quantities from the Clyde, so that by the time the Act came into operation there was something like a three years' stock, upon which no duty could be charged. Mr. Attwood had previously consulted some of the most eminent legal men in London, as to whether there was any risk in what he had done ; and the answer he got--that there was a standing order against the repeal or alteration of any fiscal bill passed in the same session of Parliament—gave him increased assurance in the course he adopted. But the Irish Ministers did not relish the turn that affairs had taken, and one of them—Mr. Fitzgerald—surreptitiously introduced into the Irish Customs Act a clause, which provided that the duty on glass should take retrospective effect. This provision was tagged on to the end of a Bill dealing with quite another subject, and it was no doubt expected that it

would pass unnoticed and unchallenged. It
did so in the House of Commons, but Mr.
Attwood, wroth at finding himself so completely and unfairly "sold," buckled on his
armour, and resolved to measure weapons
with the ministers. Having heard from Ireland that his cargoes, which had been arriving
very fast, were all confiscated by the Commissioners of Customs, and would not be given
up until the Bill making them amenable to
this huge impost had received the royal
assent, he waited upon Sir Robert Peel with
the view of uttering a remonstrance. " I
cannot," said Mr. Attwood, " allow £20,000 to
be taken out of my pocket by a fraud of this
kind." " Well," replied the secretary, " there
seems to me to be no remedy for it. I cannot help you." With that he bowed Mr. Attwood to the door, evidently annoyed, or at
any rate not prepossessed by the high ground
and unvarnished terms which his visitor had
chosen to assume. It went against his grain
to be beaten, and so Mr. Attwood, after pon-
dering in his heart, the most likely means of
checkmating the move of the Government,
took the coach and drove down into County
Wicklow, where he took the opinion of Lord
Plunkett, some time Attorney General, and a
man of profound legal acumen. His lordship
distinctly affirmed " that a retrospective
duty could not be imposed in the Queen's

courts." Armed with this opinion, Mr. Attwood once more waited upon Peel. He found the secretary stiffer and sterner than before. He would listen to nothing, and insisted that the duty should be paid. At last Mr. Attwood said " we are advised that it cannot be imposed in the Queen's courts, and we mean to try it there." " You can do as you like," said Peel, " We will be prepared to meet you." Moving to the door, Mr. Attwood added, " Before I go, I may just tell you that I hold in my hand the written opinion of Lord Plunkett, that the duty is illegal." " Wait a minute," said Peel, who became much agitated—for Lord Plunkett and he were enemies and rivals, and he was doubtless afraid that it might lead to a vote of censure —" Perhaps you will allow me to see that opinion." " Certainly, sir," said Mr. Attwood, who placed the document in the Secretary's hands, and watched his fingers nervously trying to untie the red tape ; " you can have it to sleep over if you like." Having glanced at the paper, Peel retorted, with more urbanity of manner, " This is a case of great importance. I could not give you an answer on it just now." Mr. Attwood replied that he might do so at his leisure, and retired. Before nine o'clock next morning, however, he received a note, with Mr. Secretary Peel's compliments, to the effect that "Her Majesty's

Government have resolved not to enforce the duties on window glass imposed under the recent Act of Parliament." Next session, much to Mr. Attwood's disgust and loss, Peel and Fitzgerald brought in a bill to repeal altogether the duty on window glass, and after lying for many months on the open quays at Dublin, his large stock had to be disposed of at a great sacrifice.

In the month of May, 1828, Mr. Attwood made a discovery which has a reflex influence of some little account on the industrial annals of Cleveland. The date is firmly impressed in Mr. Attwood's mind, because he was coming down from London to Northampton for the purpose of meeting a favourite blood mare of his own—the first he had entered for a race—which was to take part in the "Oaks" of that year. The mare was to come from Manchester, and Mr. Attwood, travelling from London in the mail coach—for it was in the pre-railway days—expected to meet her at Northampton. Here he slept during the night, finding that his mare had not arrived; and next morning he got up at six o'clock, with the object of having a walk through the town. Chance led him in the direction of the Castle, in the yard of which there was a low wall, built of a curious kind of stone. After carefully examining this stone, Mr. Attwood became convinced that it was iron ore,

identical in kind with that now found in Cleveland. He had previously met with the same
description of ore. During all the years he
lived in the neighbourhood of Newcastle, he
was on the outlook for minerals, having been
trained to a knowledge of metallurgy and
mineralogy; and the late Mr. John Clayton
was accustomed to show him specimens of
stone obtained from the Whitby district, that
was occasionally used in the furnaces of the
Tyne Iron Company, at Lemington. Mr.
Clayton told them with reference to this
peculiar stone—" We get it by little vessels
that go down the coast about Whitby in the
summer time, and when the tide recedes,
these vessels, lying upon the sand, are filled
with blocks of ironstone that are washed off
the cliffs on to the beach." The quantity of
stone thus obtained was very fragmentary and
precarious; and having been informed by Mr.
Clayton and others, that the Whitby stone
made bad iron *per se*, he took little further
interest in it. But he knew the deposition
of the stone thoroughly. He was aware, that
in all the other ironstone-bearing districts of
Great Britain the mineral was found in nodular
bands, whereas, here in Cleveland, it lay in
rock masses. He also believed that there was
an enormous quantity of this oolitic or Cleveland stone; and when he found it cropping
up in Northamptonshire he resolved in his

mind whether it could not be turned to good account. Northampton is about half-way between Staffordshire and London. There was a splendid highway the whole distance—commencing with the River Trent in Staffordshire, and then *viâ* the Grand Junction Canal to the Metropolis. It struck Mr. Attwood that as the heavy laden boats or barges navigating the canal came back empty, it might suit the purpose of the canal company to allow them to be charged with this ironstone as back freight, in which case it could be delivered in Staffordshire for a very small cost. Meanwhile, however, the important problem "where does this stone come from ?" presented itself for solution. He made inquiries about Northampton, and found no one who could at all throw light upon his question. All that day until sunset he walked to and fro in the neighbourhood, and as he came home he passed through a ploughed field about a mile from the town. As is the custom in the country, the hind or ploughman was unyoking his horses, leaving the plough in the furrow. Following the track of the plough, he discovered that it had been turning over iron-stone along its entire course. He asked the "yokel" about it, but could get no satisfactory idea as to what it was, or to what extent it was known to be disseminated throughout the district. He had no difficulty, however, in recognising it as identical with the stone he had seen in the Tyne, brought from Whitby. He concluded, therefore, that it would be found, more or less abundantly, scattered over the country between Northampton and Cleveland. With these conclusions in his mind, he wrote to his brother-in-law in Staffordshire— Mr. William Matthews, a well-known iron- master—"You can get oolitic ironstone here at 1s. per ton. I think it will be worth your while looking after it, for your Staffordshire ironstone is very dear." Mr. Matthews wrote back—"Even if you could guarantee me the stone at 1s. per ton it is worth nothing, for the Canal Company charge 35s. per ton for the carriage of iron to London, and it would not pay me to allow one-half that rate." Thus repulsed and disappointed, Mr. Attwood took no further notice of the discovery he had made in Northampton. The matter had indeed almost entirely passed from his memory, until one day in the spring of 1830, he was riding from Thirsk across the Hambledon Moors, to the training stables of some Arabian horses which he intended running in the " Oaks" of that year. On his way, he observed that the country roads were mended with the same oolitic ironstone that he had found at Northampton. The coincidence struck him at once, and confirmed him in the impression that the iron ore extended the length of Whitby,

and thence near to Stockton and Middlesbrough. Addressing a country man whom he
met, he asked, " Can you tell me where this
stone comes from ?" "Down that lane, sir,"
was the reply, pointing in the direction indicated. Instead, therefore, of going to the
training grounds, Mr. Attwood determined to
devote the morning to find out, if possible,
the formation of this deposit. He turned
his horse's head down the lane, and after
following its course for about a mile and a-
half, he came to a limestone quarry, used for
agricultural purposes, where there was a considerable quantity of it collected. The stone
had evidently been disinterred in building these
limekilns, and was thrown aside as useless
rubbish. Again, it occurred to Mr. Attwood,
whether his discovery could not be turned to
advantage. The railway system was then in
its infancy. Between Darlington and Stockton there was a line worked entirely by
horses. But between Manchester and Liverpool the system had been tried on the present
modern scale, and tried successfully. It therefore seemed to Mr. Attwood, that railway
facilities would soon become extensively
developed in England, and bring into close
and easy contact mineral districts, otherwise
too remote to be worked in conjunction and
inter-dependence. In view of such a probability, he began to attach great importance to

the discovery at Thirsk which could so soon
be brought into practical co-operation with
the Durham coal-field, although it could not
be opened out at that time. Another link
was soon afterwards added to the chain—this
time, also, in an accidental manner. Mr. Attwood had some shooting quarters behind
Haltwhistle, where he was accustomed to
spend some time every year. His brother-
in-law, Mr. Matthews, was as fond of grouse-
shooting as himself, and generally joined him
at Haltwhistle in the season. In August of
this same year, 1830, after they had finished
their shooting campaign together, and when
Mr. Matthews was talking about returning to
Staffordshire, Mr. Attwood said, " Do you remember me writing you three years ago about
a rock of ironstone I found at Northampton,
and which I thought might be made of some
value to you in Staffordshire?" " I recollect
perfectly," was the reply. " Then," said Mr.
Attwood, " I found that same rock close at
hand here, and rely upon it, it will be brought
into connection with the coal-field before long,
and give rise to quite a new iron trade." Mr.
Attwood then proposed that his brother-in-
law should accompany him to Thirsk, and see
the stone for himself. Mr. Matthews at once
consented. They slept at Thirsk all night,
and went on together next morning to the
training ground, stopping by the way to look
c

in upon the quarry where Mr. Attwood had found the ironstone. Mr. Matthews was much struck with the discovery, and filled his shooting-jacket pockets with specimens of the stone, which he intended to take with him to Staffordshire for the purpose of analysis.

We are now approaching the beginning of the end of this part of our narrative. Mr. Attwood waited for the railway system to bring the Durham coal-field and the Cleveland ironstone together, satisfied that when that union had been completed there would be an immense impetus given to the Northern iron and coal trades. While he lived in London he became a subscriber to the first geological map that was ever published. It was drawn up by William Smith, the geologist —a relative of Professor Philips, the mineralogist, of Oxford, and the discoverer of the regular order of superposition of the British strata. Smith had prepared a complete geological map of England, but it was too bulky a thing for general use, and it was therefore determined to carry out a scheme of publishing separate geological maps for each county. Geology was then less understood and appreciated than it is at the present day, and after twelve county maps had been published the scheme had to be abandoned for want of adequate support. But, fortunately, the map of Yorkshire was one of the twelve

—indeed, it was the very last published—and a wonderful map it is for the accuracy of its outlines. Mr. Attwood instructed his nephew to make out a copy of Smith's map on a small scale, and added, "We will go next week and trace this ironstone from Scarborough to the Tees; and as soon as we come to Middlesbrough we shall find its main seam either here (putting his finger on Eston Nab), or here (pointing to Roseberry Topping). The bed is in the lias limestone formation, and wherever it is laid bare under the oolitic, all the way down to the mouth of the Severn, that bed exists." Mr. Attwood's nephew prepared the map as desired. The writer has been permitted to examine it, as well as a copy of the geological survey for Yorkshire, prepared by Smith, which shows a section of the coast from Scarborough up to the mouth of the Tees. At this time the railway had just been opened from Stockton to Middlesbrough, and Mr. Attwood had made up his mind to acquire a large royalty of the Cleveland ironstone, and commence the manufacture of iron in that district.

It was at this juncture that circumstances occurred which directed Mr. Attwood's thoughts into quite another channel, and prevented him from taking the position which has since, by universal assent, been awarded to Mr. John Vaughan. It was Burns who wrote—

"The best laid schemes o' men and mice
   Gang aft agley;"

and so it was with the plans of Mr. Attwood.
Before he had time to carry out his contem-
plated examination of the Cleveland hills, he
was waited upon by a man named Walton,
who had formerly owned a small freehold
estate in Weardale, of which he was a native,
but at that time kept a public-house in or
near Newgate Street, Newcastle. Walton,
while working some lead mines in Weardale, came upon a peculiar mineral of which
he knew nothing, but knowing Mr. Attwood to be a mineralogist, he brought the
stone under his notice. Mr. Attwood at
once pronounced it to be a very rich and
peculiar quality of iron ore—a carbonate of
iron which was not known to exist anywhere
in Great Britain except Cornwall, although
it had been found in abundance among the
Styrian and Carinthian Alps from the time
of the Romans. In order to have his impressions fully verified, Mr. Attwood advised
Walton to send the mineral to Dr. Fyfe, of
Edinburgh, the eminent chemist, for the purpose of analysis. Walton did so, and Dr. Fyfe's
assay fully bore out the opinions of Mr. Attwood, who, having ascertained that a railway was then in course of formation which
would connect the Bishop Auckland coal-field
with Weardale, determined to turn his views

for the time being in that direction. The
district had access with the Tyne by the Weardale, Stanhope, and Tyne Railway—the first
line constructed by Stephenson—which was
worked, not by locomotives, but by horses
and inclined planes. Having revolved in his
own mind the all-important question of railway facilities, Mr. Attwood said to Walton,
" You know Weardale very well; do you think
there is much of this stuff? " " Yes," he replied, " I'm of opinion that there's a very large
quantity of it; but it has hitherto been
thrown out of the mines as useless." " Then,
we'll go through the valley and see what
quantity of it can be got ; it's a stone of some
value." With Walton as their guide, Mr.
Attwood and his nephew made a tour of the
lead mines, and found that large quantities
of the "rider ore" had been cast out of the
mines as rubbish, its tendency being injurious
to the lead with which it is found in combination. Mr. Attwood knew that if he could
obtain a sufficient quantity of this ore, he
would be able to produce the best iron made
in Britain ; while he also knew that the Cleveland ore made a very inferior quality of iron.
He did not like the idea of making bad iron,
no matter what its commercial results might
be, so he elected to throw in his lot with the
Weardale ores, saying to his nephew and himself, " We'll let Cleveland alone in the mean-

time; it will keep perhaps long enough." These circumstances led to the abandonment of the proposed survey of the Cleveland hills, and involved, as its necessary corollary, the loss of prestige Mr. Attwood would undoubtedly have gained had he followed up his discoveries and intentions.

The next matter that claimed Mr. Attwood's attention was the acquisition of a lease for working the "rider ore" of Weardale. He ascertained that the lead mines of Weardale had been held for many generations by the Blackett family, which subsequently merged in that of Beaumont. And it may be noticed, *en passant*, that two centuries previously a Mr. Edward Blackett, the owner of the few lead mines worked in the district at that remote period, had been known to have worked Weardale iron ore, which was made into iron and steel by a small colony of Germans on the Derwent. The works were carried on at Shotley Bridge, near Consett where their remains may be traced to this day; while the descendants of these German steelworkers may still be identified in the neighbourhood by their queer-sounding names. In those days the art of making iron and steel with coal or coke was quite unknown. Charcoal was the only fuel used, and as the supply of wood in the district became scarce, the steel works were abandoned. Returning from this digression, we find that a gentleman of the name of Pearson, an agent of the Bishop of Durham, had taken, on speculation, a lease of the iron ore in the manors of Stanhope and Wolsingham, at a merely nominal rent, a number of years previous to Walton's discovery. Mr. Pearson had only one child—a daughter, who married the late Mr. George Hutton Wilkinson, some time recorder of Newcastle, and through her the lease reverted to her husband and family. But by them the value and character of the iron ore in Weardale appeared only to be guessed at. Most of those to whom Mr. Attwood spoke on the subject were quite incredulous of the existence of such ore. One old man knowingly declared, "Nay ; that's no ironstone ; it's only brunt (burnt) stuff." But Mr. Attwood persisted that it was ironstone of the finest quality ; and, unwisely for himself perhaps, made a good deal of noise about it, for when he went to see Mr. Wilkinson about entering into a lease, he found that Mr. Cuthbert Rippon had been there a few days before him, and had just arranged for the working of all the ironstone in the two manors of Stanhope and Wolsingham. Under the circum-, stances, Mr. Attwood was compelled to make arrangements with Mr. Rippon for a sub-lease of the manor on much less advantageous terms than he could have made with Mr. Wilkinson, had he kept his own counsel.

Having thus established himself in Weardale, Mr. Attwood built five blast furnaces at Tow Law, and purchased another, which Mr. Rippon had erected at Stanhope. His expectations as to the quality of iron that could be produced from the so-called "rider ore" were amply verified. No less an authority than Mr. Isaac Lowthian Bell has declared that the iron made at Tow Law is of a very high class—so good, indeed, as closely to resemble in quality the celebrated German "Spiegeleisen." For bar iron purposes it bears a high name, and has, like its prototype in Germany, been found pre-eminently well adapted for the manufacture of the finer kinds of steel—an application confined exclusively to the purest descriptions of metal. Meanwhile, Messrs. Bolckow and Vaughan had built three blast furnaces at Witton Park, relying upon their ability to procure adequate supplies of stone in that district. Herein they were grievously disappointed. They experienced the utmost difficulty in obtaining ironstone sufficient to keep their furnaces blowing, and in their dilemma Mr. Vaughan called on Mr. Attwood, and asked for a supply of his Weardale ores. The latter was unable to spare any of the "rider ore," which is not found in great beds like the Cleveland stone, but in isolated patches, very irregular and precarious. In the neighbourhood of

Consett, however, he had leased a large royalty of clayband ironstone, from which he furnished Messrs. Bolckow and Vaughan with occasional supplies.   Things were in this state when, one day in the spring of 1850, Mr. Vaughan paid a visit to Mr. Attwood at Tow Law.   After some general conversation Mr. Vaughan said, " I've come to sell you some ironstone."   "Indeed," replied Mr. Attwood, who could scarcely conceal his astonishment, " I'm sorry to hear that, for I expected you had come to buy some from me. However," he added, " if you can sell me iron-stone cheaper and better than I can work it for myself, I'll be your customer.   What can you deliver it for at Tow Law?"   "Six shillings a ton," said Mr. Vaughan.   Mr. Attwood at once jumped to the conclusion that the Cleveland ironstone, which he had imagined was yet unknown, had at last been found out.   Without expressing his thoughts, however, he asked, "In what part of the country do you find stone that you can deliver at 6s per ton?"   In an off-hand way, Mr. Vaughan replied, " On the railway close by Darlington."   Mr. Attwood was not to be misled by this ambiguous reply.   He went to a drawer, pulled out the geological maps to which allusion has already been made, spread them out before his visitor and said: " Now, I know the geology of Darlington very well;

there's no stone to be found thereabouts. At one or other of these places (putting his fingers on the spots indicating Roseberry Topping and Eston Nab) you must find your ironstone." "Mr. Vaughan," said Mr. Attwood, when relating the anecdote to the writer, "looked at me as if I had been a witch." Admitting the truth of what Mr. Attwood had affirmed, he added, "We've not concluded our arrangements yet; and we dont want it to be known." "All right," was the reply, "you need not fear me. I advise you to go on, for you've got hold of a good thing."

Although the events already recorded prevented him from taking up the position to which he had looked forward—that of being the first to demonstrate the practical value of the Cleveland ironstone—Mr. Attwood was not prepared to relinquish altogether his long cherished intention of some day obtaining a footing in the Cleveland district. He, therefore, about the beginning of 1852, began to look out for ironstone royalties near to Eston. But Messrs. Bolckow and Vaughan on the one side, and the Consett Iron Company on the other, had pretty much taken up the first range of hills. Dissappointed thereat, Mr. Attwood still argued "I cannot afford to lose it; I must secure some of this stone before it is all eaten up." At last he was able to conclude negotiations for the lease of a royalty of some 5,000 acres near to Guisborough. In this venture he was joined by his partners in the Weardale works—the Messrs. Baring, of London. But they, as bankers, knew nothing of the merits of the Cleveland stone, and as, on inquiry, they heard unfavourable accounts of it, they dissuaded Mr. Attwood from attempting its development. This was done much against Mr. Attwood's own inclinations, for he had a strong presentiment that Cleveland was the place in which to make money rapidly, there being always a ready market for cheap goods, and Mr. Vaughan had told him that his firm could make iron from Cleveland ore for 25s per ton. He had his hands almost full in Weardale, however, and on this account he allowed his own predilections to be overruled by the prejudices of his partners. The result was that the Guisborough royalty remained almost untouched for a number of years. The trade being in its infancy, the market was restricted; and most of the new firms who came into the district to build blast furnaces did so by arrangement with the Messrs. Pease, of Darlington, who gave them railway facilities which Mr. Attwood and his partners were not in a position to offer.

At last, in the year 1870, two blast furnaces each 85 feet in height, were erected at Tudhoe, (where the Company had previously, in

1852, established rolling mills and forges) for smelting the Cleveland ironstone. The " make " of these furnaces averages about 800 tons per week. The output from the Weardale Company's mines in Cleveland is now at the rate of 400,000 tons per annum. Since they acquired their royalty, the Company have disposed of over 2,000 acres stretching away in the direction of Thirsk, to which Mr. Attwood did not attach much value. But they have still about 3,000 acres of the best stone under lease—and the bed is so thick that, as Mr. Attwood has himself put it, " We could almost supply a hundred blast furnaces, if we had them, for as many years."

In addition to their Tow Law works, where there are five blast furnaces, erected in 1847, and each forty-eight feet in height, the Weardale Company have Bessemer works at Tudhoe, in which a great part of the iron made at Tow Law is converted into steel. This branch of their operations has a most interesting history, upon which we may be excused for briefly dwelling, seeing that it has not hitherto been told. Mr. Attwood was the first to take a license from Bessemer, who, at the time he brought out his patent, carried on an establishment at Sheffield. Having heard from the patentee of the new invention, Mr. Attwood made a trial of it, and was favourably impressed with the results, although they were not quite perfect. He thought it worth while, however, to see his partners, and elicit their opinion as to taking a license. The reply he got was, " Better let it alone ; we don't know anything about it." Just at this juncture a rather curious incident occurred, which, trifling in itself, led, nevertheless to most important results. The manager of the Weardale Company's rolling mills, at Tud-hoe, who had little faith in Bessemer's process, was one day travelling on the railway, when he met Mr. William Bird, a leading authority in the iron trade, long resident in London. Bird, who was a friend of the patentee said, " I want somebody who will work steel for Bessemer. Will you undertake it at Tudhoe ?" The manager replied that they would be glad to do so for a fair price. " Well," retorted Bird, " what we specially require is to make ship plates—say about six hundred tons per week. It will require good strong works, and I think yours will suit." " All right," said the other, "we'll make any quantity you like for £6 per ton." It was ultimately agreed that Bessemer would send ingots from his works at Sheffield to Tudhoe, and that they were to be manufactured into ship plates at the latter works. Mr. Attwood's manager predicted it would be an utter failure. Mr. Attwood himself held quite a different opinion, and stuck to it. At last a cargo of twenty tons of steel ingots was delivered at Tudhoe, and Mr. Bessemer appeared in person to watch operations. Mr. Attwood was also present, and took much interest in the experiments, which proved so successful that Mr. Bessemer almost induced Mr. Attwood to purchase a license to work the new patent. Before doing so, however, Mr. Attwood sent his manager over to Sheffield that he might see the process carried on in Mr. Bessemer's own works. "I have altered my views entirely," wrote the manager a day or two afterwards, "Bessemer has now overcome all his difficulties, and can make steel of a uniform and workable quality. The thing is now worth looking after." Anxious, however, still further to test the merits of the process, Mr. Attwood went over to Sheffield himself, taking with him twenty tons of Weardale iron. At Mr. Bessemer's works he stayed for a week, closely scrutinising the effects of the new process on his own iron, and was so satisfied with the result that he at once undertook to purchase a license. It was about this time that Bessemer was threatened with litigation that might have involved the invalidity of his patent. Mushet, a relative of the discoverer of the Scotch "black band" ironstone, had brought out a great many patents, and one of them proposed to deal with the manufacture of steel by a process which in some respects resembled that patented by Bessemer. While this ugly case was pending, Mr. Attwood met Bessemer and told him that his was a precarious patent, for, he added, " I see you are under the lash of Mushet, and I don't like the idea of having to pay twice over for my license." " Well," said Mr. Bessemer, " I can assure you it is quite a mistake to say that we are using Mushet's patent; we are getting iron from Sweden that keeps us safe." "That may be," said Mr. Attwood, "but if I go on with this license you must guarantee me against all risk so far as Mushet is concerned." Bessemer gave the required undertaking, but when he saw Mr. Attwood proceeding to lay down a plant costing over £10,000, on a plan furnished by himself—the patentee—he seemed to be somewhat doubtful about the wisdom of what he had done. Shortly afterwards, however, Mr. Attwood had another visit from Bessemer, whose first news was— " All danger is now past, for Mushet has allowed his patent to lapse for want of paying the patent fees." " It is impossible," replied Mr. Attwood, " that he can have been such a fool." " It's nevertheless a fact, though," said the emancipated patentee, " for my agent, having satisfied himself of its accuracy, hurried down to tell me." Meanwhile, the

Bessemer works at Tudhoe had been finished; and it was found that there was something radically faulty about them. It was one thing to make ingots, but it was quite another thing to forge and roll them. Mr. Attwood could not personally give much attention to the matter, for he was at this time an infirm valetudinarian, and unable to undertake the daily fatigue of travelling between Wolsingham, where he resided and Tudhoe—a distance of fifteen miles. Experience, however, ultimately enabled the more serious faults of the process to be corrected, and it is in successful operation at Tudhoe to this day. His process has realised a princely fortune for Mr. Bessemer, while it has entirely revolutionised the steel manufacture of Great Britain, enabling steel bars—which formerly cost £40 to £50 per ton—to be made at a selling price of about £11 per ton, after paying the royalty fee of £2.

The last phase of Mr. Attwood's industrial career to which we propose to allude is his own invention for the manufacture of steel. He patented this curious discovery about the year 1862. Satisfied of its merits and commercial value, he proposed to his partners to take it up and work it on a large scale. They again withheld their consent, remarking complacently, " Well, we daresay you are right; but we don't understand your process, and we have a natural dislike to anything we cannot comprehend." Mr. Attwood replied, "Having made this singular invention, I mean to perfect it, and if you don't care to go along with me, I shall do it myself." At that time, however, he was in very feeble health. His medical advisers told him that if he would live for a few years longer he must select a warmer climate. Mr. Attwood reluctantly consented to visit the south, and he spent the most of next summer at Torquay, returning to Wolsingham much benefited by the change. He then arranged with his nephew to go into his new steel manufacture thoroughly. Land was acquired for the purpose, within a short distance of his house at Wolsingham ; but the foundations of the new works had hardly been laid when Mr. Attwood's nephew was prostrated by paralysis, and in a year more he joined the great majority. It was a severe blow to Mr. Attwood, who had no family of his own, and to whom his nephew was all but a son. He relaxed his interest in his new steel process, and although the proposed works were built, it was on a smaller scale than that originally intended. Part of the first lot of steel rails made by Mr. Attwood's process was sent to London, where six different railway companies exposed them to the severest tests by putting them down in the most trying places. These rails are as good

to-day as they were when first put down.
Two years ago, Mr. Attwood said to the railway companies " You have already reported
favourably on my rails. Why not take a lot
of say 200 tons, and let us have a fuller
trial ?" In reply to this invitation, the Great
Northern Railway Company at once sent an
order for 250 tons, and added, " We will take
as much more as you like to make. The way
in which your rails stand is perfectly wonderful." In about three years time, Mr. Attwood's patent will expire. The merits of his
invention will then become more fully known,
and the patentee is sanguine enough to expect
that firms who have spent a great deal of
money in laying down Bessemer plant will
discard the one system in favour of the other.
It is no secret that Bessemer plates are
defective in flexibility, which makes them
liable to break in hot weather by the action
of the sun's heat. Mr. Attwood thinks he has
overcome this difficulty. Some of his more
recent orders refer to the application of steel
to masts for large steamers. Whatever may
be the value of his process, it has been a source
of little or no emolument to Mr. Attwood
himself, for he has never followed it out so as
to make it a great commercial success. It
will probably be left for others to reap what
he has sown.

The trial of Queen Caroline in the year

1820 was the first event that drew Mr. Attwood from the retirement of private life. In common with all his countrymen, Mr. Attwood's feelings were strongly excited by the result of that trial. He felt that the Queen was the victim of an infamous prosecution, and that she was treated with less than justice, in order to satisfy the caprice of her licentious and abandoned husband. Knowing something of the value of the Italian evidence on which the prosecution chiefly relied to establish proof of the Queen's adultery, Mr. Attwood opened up communication with Mr. Denman, her Solicitor-General. In Mr. Brougham, her Attorney-General, he had little faith, believing that he trimmed to please both George and Caroline, and that his advocacy of the Queen's cause was only half-hearted. In his business relations Mr. Attwood had experienced the mendacity of Italian testimony, and he was prepared to demonstrate to the Queen's counsel the utter rottenness and want of veracity which were characteristic of such evidence; but Mr. Denman hesitated to take advantage of his proferred services, and the "*non mi ricordo*" testimony of Tacodor Mejocchi and his companions, was thus allowed to appear on the record, when it might at the outset have been completely discredited. The trial meanwhile proceeded, and the whole country was roused to a sense of indignation

at the treatment to which the unhappy Queen
was exposed. When the Bill of "Pains and
Penalties" was introduced by Lord Liverpool
"to deprive her Majesty Queen Caroline
Amelia Elizabeth of the title, prerogatives,
rights, and privileges of Queen Consort of
this realm, and to dissolve the marriage between his Majesty and the said Caroline
Amelia Elizabeth," the nation cried "shame!"
and excitement bordered on revolution. Both
Whigs and Tories were eager partizans of her
Majesty; but, curiously enough, although the
question of a divorce had been long enough
before the country, the cardinal point involved
in the case had hitherto escaped public attention. As her Majesty's Attorney-General
afterwards pointed out, it was provided by
the Standing Orders of the House of Lords
"that the husband who applies for a divorce
shall personally attend the House, so that he
may be examined before the divorce is granted,
in order to show that there is no collusion,
that he stands *rectus in curia*, and that he himself, having always stood as a kind and faithful husband, is entitled to a dissolution of
marriage by reason of the infidelity of his
wife." George IV. did not come into court
with clean hands; and, therefore, he could
not, except by a subversion of the principles
that had always guided the House of Lords,
and a prostitution of its functions, secure the

separation he desired. Carlton House was
an asylum for harlots. The King's whole career, both antecedent and subsequent to his
marriage with Caroline was profligate and im-
moral in the extreme. Yet there seemed to be
a majority of the Lords ready to support the
Bill of "Pains and Penalties," and although the
feeling in the Queen's favour was gathering
strength out of doors, it was fully expected that
the divorce would be granted. At this crisis
Mr. Attwood threw himself into the agitation.
He had not made up his mind that the Queen
was all that she should be, but he had abundant reason to believe that the King was a
bad man, and that he was treating his wife
unfairly. Sitting in his office in London one
day, revolving the case in his own mind, he
was led to pen a glowing and powerful
letter to the *Times*, in which he pointed out
that the King had no *locus standi* by reason of
his own misdeeds, and predicted the terribly
disastrous consequences that would ensue if
the House of Lords exercised their preroga-
tive in defiance of old-established orders, and
granted a divorce against the universal
sympathies of the nation. This letter he entrusted to a messenger, who assisted him in
his laboratory experiments, to take to the
office of the " Thunderer," enjoining him to
wait and take back the manuscript if it was
rejected. The communication was scanned by

the editor, who at once returned the message, "Tell Mr. Attwood that it shall appear to-morrow." Next day Mr. Attwood's letter not only appeared in leading type in a prominent part of the paper, but there was also an "editorial" homologating all that the letter contained. It was the custom in those days for the leaders of public opinion, both in Parliament and in the press, to send out spies throughout the city to test the tendencies of the popular feeling in reference to any subject before the country. One of these emissaries in the pay of the Earl of Lonsdale (who then occupied a high place in the counsels of the Conservative party) visited Mr. Attwood on the morning that this letter made its appearance. He declared that his master and his friends thoroughly approved of its tone, and that it had set the whole city by the ears. Letter and leader together swayed public opinion to such an extent that when the Bill of "Pains and Penalties" came up for discussion their Lordships refused to pass it, thus preventing the succession to the Crown from being transferred into another and an improper line.

During the ten years that elapsed between 1820 and 1830, Mr. Attwood took little part in political life. But circumstances occurred in the latter year that again brought him to the front. The accession of William IV. led

to a general election, and Lord Campbell, in
his "Lives of the Chancellors," tells us that
" before the hustings were erected, suddenly
there arose all over the kingdom, in the place
of apathy and indifference, a state of almost
unexampled excitement." This was caused by
the great revolution in Paris, which exiled the
elder branch of the Bourbons, and placed
Louis Philippe, " the Citizen King," upon the
throne. Englishmen seemed to awaken from
torpor to the sudden belief that they were
slaves. No imported plague ever produced
such rapid effects or spread so widely.
There was then a great deal of destitution
among the agricultural peasantry of the
southern counties, which, taken in conjunction
with the " new-fangled" doctrines of " liberty,
equality, and fraternity" brought over from
France, made them discontented and recalcit-
rant. They made demonstrations of an
aggressive character, and clamoured loudly
for greater consideration and justice. Mr.
Attwood used to describe this rising as the
rebellion of " ash sticks and hazel wands ;"
but the Government of Earl Grey took a much
more serious view of the matter, and caused
many of the ringleaders to be apprehended
and cast into prison. Pending their trial,
Cobbett announced through his *Political
Register* that it was the intention of the Government to put thirty of these quiet, simple,

and honest peasantry to death. This news
fired Mr. Attwood's blood. He knew what the
agricultural peasantry were. He felt that it
would be a flagrant iniquity if the intention
of the Government was carried into effect, for
they were not now dealing with hardened and
dangerous ruffians, but with decent, law-
abiding, industrious men, who, in his view,
had only too much reason for the riot in which
they took part. He determined to make an
effort to save the lives of the doomed men.
He was impelled to this course by the most
tender and loving memories of others of their
class. One old man, who had been in his
father's employment as an agricultural
labourer for fifty-two years, remarked to
him at the funeral of his sire, " I shall miss
him, Charles, more, perhaps, than you. I
have been with him in all the circumstances
of life. He was aye a good master to me, and
now that he is dead I don't feel that I have
anything to live for." It was with such reminiscences as this, that Mr. Attwood was
accustomed to associate the character of the
rural peasantry of the south ; and it is little
wonder, therefore, that he was full of indignation when he heard of the example that Government intended to make of the rioters who
had been placed upon their trial. On Saturday afternoon, while musing over their fate,
he determined to draw up a petition for their

more lenient treatment. No time was to be
lost. He composed the petition hastily, but
earnestly, hurried into Newcastle, and put it
into the hands of Mackenzie, the printer. It
was out in the streets in the course of the evening, and when it was taken up at ten o'clock
it had received no less than 3,800 signatures.
Other petitions to the same effect were sent
up from other parts of the country, and the Government was thus so far induced to alter its
original decision that only one of the rioters
was condemned to capital punishment. A
number of others were transported, but were
allowed a few years later, mainly through the
influence of Mr. Attwood's brother, to return
to their native land.

To give anything like an exhaustive account
of the political career of Mr. Attwood would
be to write a complete history of the agitation
that culminated in the passing of the Reform
Bill of 1832. Into that agitation he threw
himself heart and soul. He was in all the
counsels of the Birmingham and North of
England Political Unions. He was one of
the most effective speakers at many of
the monster meetings held up and down
the country for the promotion of the objects of the new league. In this cause he was
associated with some of the most eminent
men of the time. When the Reformers had
come within sight of the objects for which

they fought, their Union was allowed to lapse.
But the ministry of the Duke of Wellington
would not take a warning. They introduced
some unpopular measures, and made themselves otherwise obnoxious. Wroth at the
conduct of the Tories, Mr. Attwood and his
friends said, " We must re-organize the Union
again," and they did so. A great demonstra-
tion was to be held in Birmingham to initiate
this second campaign. The Duke of Wellington rightly feared a serious disturbance and
ordered the military to be called out. When
this announcement was made, a military
friend of the people sympathisingly remarked
to Attwood, " We've been ordered to sharpen
our sabres, but by G— we won't use them."
The crisis came at last. The populace of Birmingham were about to be charged by the
soldiery, when Mr. Attwood and his brother
—who will be well remembered by veteran
Reformers—were asked to interpose. " If
anybody could pacify the mob of Birmingham,"
says Mr. Attwood, " it was my brother
Thomas." That day, at least, he succeeded
in preventing bloodshed, although in subsequently passing through the streets he was
subjected to a gross outrage. At a meeting
afterwards held in Newcastle, presided over
by Mr. Attwood, one firebrand came forward
and asked " if the people were tame and das-
tardly enough to allow themselves to be

governed by a girl of eighteen ?" This sally
was received with a good deal of favour by
the meeting, but it called down a rebuke from
Mr. Attwood, who said, "I shall go any length
in the way of reforming clear and proven
abuses, but I shall not go further, and I shall
seek to discourage everybody else from going
further." "You may say what you like,"
said the other speaker, who was an Irishman,
"but I have now got my union, and —— me
if I don't baptise it in blood." Mr. Attwood
replied, "You may baptise your own union in
blood if you will, but you will not baptise
mine." Mr. Attwood had pledged himself to
reorganise the Union, but finding that reform
was now bordering on revolution, he shrunk
from the task. "I see," he said, "that there
is a growing spirit of Republicanism, and I
am not a Republican—except in the sense
that George Washington was one." The
following night he attended a meeting at
Gateshead, where the fiery Irishman again
appeared, bearing a number of placards intended to foment sedition. Here he again
declared that he could not go further with the
objects of the Union—that he could work
no longer with the men who had been his
compatriots so long, if such shibboleths as
these were to be adopted. He completely
won the approval of the audience, and his
Irish friend had to beat an ignominious re-

treat. But from this time forward, Mr. Attwood was less conspicuously mixed up with political agitations than he had previously been.

It is a somewhat remarkable fact that Mr. Attwood never sat in Parliament. He was frequently entreated to become a candidate for Parliamentary honours, but only once did he allow himself to be put in nomination. This was in the election of 1832, when he stood for Newcastle in opposition to Mr. John Hodgson Hinde, the Conservative candidate. It was at the last moment that Mr. Attwood was earnestly requested by his party to allow himself to be put forward. He only issued his address on the Saturday night, and the election was to take place on the Tuesday following. At the nomination on Monday, Mr. Attwood obtained the show of hands in his favour, and the result of the poll gave 1,200 votes for the popular candidate, and 1,500 for Mr. Hinde.

Although he has been for so many years out of the arena of political strife, Mr. Attwood has never ceased to take a lively interest in political men and measures, and he forms very pronounced opinions on both. He is a close reasoner, and an original thinker, and in the prime of manhood, he was a fluent and effective speaker. Even now, when he is all but confined to his room, and upwards of eighty years of age, he can talk for hours on the questions of the day. It is a treat of no common order to hear "the old man eloquent" discourse on some favourite theme—his eyes glistening with unwonted animation as, in imagination, he " fights his battles o'er again." There is no halting in his speech—no want of connection in his thoughts—no apparent failure of the memory. He has a wonderfully correct remembrance of names and dates. It is not, however, until he commences to criticise the public men of his day that he really approaches his former self. Of Sir Robert Peel we need hardly say he had the poorest possible opinion ; and it is a curious fact that until the day of Peel's death, he lived in the hope of again measuring weapons with him in the House of Commons or elsewhere. Neither has he much praise for Gladstone, whose speeches, he says, are like lawyers' briefs, and want the touch of genius and absence of severe mental discipline that are characteristic of the true orator. Disraeli, on the other hand, stands high in his esteem—less for his political principles than for his rare endowments.

Little remains to be added. Almost dead to the world for many years past,.Mr. Attwood has lived at his finely situated residence at Wolsingham. The last time he took part in any public event was, we believe, on the occasion of the South Durham election of

1865. Nor does he receive many visitors, for most of his old friends have pre-deceased him, and he is without many near relatives. Yet he continues withal to be very cheerful, attending regularly to business matters, and doing the bulk of his own correspondence. With the exception of a little deafness, he is in the full use of all his faculties. He may still be said to live, move, and think in an atmosphere of science. He has a very choice collection of geological specimens, in which he takes a great interest. But his steel works at Wolsingham are his chief scientific solace and recreation. He carries them on mainly as a labour of love, for, he says, " I have as much money as I really want, and I have no desire for more." One who has known him long and intimately remarked to the writer, " If Charles Attwood had cared more about money and less about science he would to-day have been one of the richest commoners in England." Take him for all in all, Charles Attwood may be described as a great and a good man—one who has been a benefactor to his race, and whose conduct has uniformly been governed by pure, philanthropic, and unselfish motives.

II.—H. W. F. BOLCKOW, M.P.

Next to practical or experimental knowledge, financial skill and administrative ability are the most essential conditions to success in a great commercial undertaking, no matter what its nature may be. For want of these primary desiderata many promising concerns, that had no end of both theoretical and practical experience behind them, have come to grief. Instances of this fact might easily be multiplied. Not a few newspaper ventures, to borrow an illustration from our own sphere, have gone to the wall because there was not in the management commercial skill commensurate with the literary genius that animated their pages, and should have ensured ultimate triumph. And, taking a leap from the Fourth to the Third Estate, we all know that the British Constitution has on more than one occasion almost suffered shipwreck because a weak and incapable Chancellor was at the helm of the Exchequer. It is this necessity for a combination of gifts, seldom found united in the same individual that has given rise to the well known aphorism " Two heads are better than one;" and of more colossal and prosperous undertakings than even Bolckow and Vaughan, it may be predicated with certainty that had one endeavoured to carry out what it required both to achieve, consummate failure would have been the result. Blending together their varied talents and attainments, Messrs. Bolckow and Vaughan exhibited a rare conjunction of aptitude and fitness for the enterprise on which they embarked. The one had capital; the other was without, but supplied what was equally valuable and indispensible—skilled labour and experience. The one was an adept in the management of figures; the other had a genius for the government of men. The one knew little or nothing about the scientific and practical details of their enterprise; the other knew more than most men, and had a capacity for turning his knowledge to good account. Thus it came about that the one supplied the motive power and the other actuated it. In all their relations there was an interdependence which both felt to be necessary to their mutual benefit. It is no limitation of the credit due to Mr. Vaughan, nor yet a reflection on his capacity to say that, without Mr. Bolckow's counsel and co-operation, he could never have taken

the position he did, so that although different
opinions may prevail as to the exact degree
of merit and honour attaching to each, (and
this is really in itself a matter of little importance), all will agree in allowing Mr.
Bolckow a prominent position alongside that
of his partner, as a pioneer of the North of
England iron tade.

Henry William Ferdinand Bolckow, son
of a country gentleman, is a native of Sulten,
in Mecklenburg, a Grand Duchy of North
Germany, where he was born in the year
1806. It is mostly an agricultural country,
the chief exports being grain, rape seeds, and
other produce of the soil, so that it offers few
facilities or inducements for a commercial
career. He commenced his career in a merchant's office at Rostock, and after having been
there for several years, on the invitation of
his friend, Mr. C. Allhusen, Mr. Bolckow went
to Newcastle-on-Tyne, in 1827, and ultimately
joined him in his business of a general commission merchant in that town. Although
this would have satisfied many men, as a
congenial spbere of labour and a promising outlet for capital, Mr. Bolckow, after
some years, felt inclined to change for a
business occupation of a more steady
character, and having made the acquaintance of Mr. Vaughan, whom he knew
to possess a thoroughly practical knowledge

E

of iron manufacture, he dissolved partnership with Mr. Allhusen, and, along with Mr.
Vaughan, decided to establish iron works.
On the advice of the late Mr. John Harris, who
was the engineer of the Stockton and Darlington Railway, they selected Middlesbrough,
a place then scarcely known, for their
venture. As we have already indicated, Mr.
Bolckow was the capitalist, having at his disposal a fortune of £40,000 to £50,000, while
his partner had not as many hundreds; but as
the one was indispensable to the other, it was
agreed that they should go shares in everything. On Mr. Bolckow's part it was a bold
—some might even call it a rash—speculation.
He was in a safe, if somewhat slow and steady
line of business at Newcastle; the industrial
resources of the Cleveland district had not then
been discovered, much less tested and proved;
and of the business on which he was about to
embark he knew little or nothing. Nor was
there anything about Cleveland, as it was
known at that time, offering any special inducements for its selection as their future
sphere of operations. It had shipping facilities, no doubt, and was within easy access of
the Durham coal fields; but the same could
be said of Sunderland, Shields, Newcastle,
Hartlepool, and some other ports on the east
coast, where the firm might, with as much
apparent advantage, have " pitched their

tent." Was it a merely fortuitous chain of
events that led to the selection of Middlesbrough, or was the choice inspired by a
dream of the rich mineral treasures that surrounded that insignificant little town ? It is
difficult to believe that chance, and chance
alone, guided their movements ; and yet we
are confronted with the perplexing fact, that
whereas they came to Middlesbrough in 1841,
the main seam of the Cleveland ironstone was
not discovered until eight years later, nor was
its adaptibility for blast furnace purposes acknowledged until the firm had been nine or ten
years in existence. Had it been otherwise, the
firm would undoubtedly have turned its knowledge to practical account before they did.

In our sketch of Mr. Vaughan's career, we
trace the progress of this eminent firm up
to the period of the opening of the Eston
mines in 1850. That event led almost immediately to a great and rapid development
of the iron trade of Cleveland. And it is now
a well known fact, that it brought about an
enormous extension of the trade and population, as well as the subsequent prosperity of
Middlesbrough and the surrounding district,
benefiting alike railway companies, land and
coal owners, and all classes of the population.
The creation of this enormous trade and
industry is certainly due to Bolckow and
Vaughan, and the importance of it may be

estimated from the fact, that the quantity of Pig Iron produced from Cleveland Stone is about two millions of tons per annum at present. In 1852 Messrs. Bolckow and Vaughan built three blast furnaces at Middlesbrough, and in the following year, they built six furnaces at Eston, only two miles from their mines, to which a branch railway was laid. They had, as far back as 1845, erected four blast furnaces at Witton Park, and ultimately they acquired the Cleveland Ironworks, consisting of three furnaces, and built by Elwon and Company in 1854. By this time their operations were on quite a gigantic scale. They continued to multiply their resources until the year 1865, when the works were transferred to a Limited Liability Company, with a capital of two and a-half millions sterling, in shares of nominally £100 each. For years past the market value of these shares has fluctuated between £40 and £50 premium, and has several times touched the latter figure. The present price of the shares of £35—and including Bonus Shares of £30—is about £115. Mr. Bolckow is chairman of the company, and the general manager is Mr. Edward Williams, another self-made man like Mr. Vaughan, having, like him, commenced life in an ironworks, and possessing much of his shrewdness, energy of character, and ample experience. For the last four or five years this great Company have consumed annually between 700,000 and 800,000 tons of ironstone, nearly 300,000 tons of coke, 150,000 to 160,000 tons of limestone, and 300,000 tons of coal. Upwards of 230,000 tons of pig iron are produced annually, in addition to 80,000 to 100,000 tons of finished iron, 30,000 tons of castings, and a variety of general engineering work. The company own about a dozen collieries, from which they raise about 1,000,000 tons of coal per annum; they farm several thousand acres of land; they own hematite ironstone mines in Spain, Africa, and Portugal; and they keep a fleet of steamers conveying the ore between their foreign mines and Middlesbrough. They also own steel works at Manchester of considerable extent. At their Middlesbrough works the company manufacture their own gas, and build their own engines and wagons; while as a further example of the magnitude of their ramifications, it may be stated that they make the fire bricks used in the construction of their furnaces. Altogether, their works give employment to about 10,000 hands.

These stupendous results were not attained without passing through the vicissitudes that attend all industrial enterprises to a greater or less extent, and Mr. Bolckow, whose business it was to provide the means wherewith to carry on the firm, found more than once that the tide of adversity was almost too

strong for them. Yet through his firmness
and determination to carry on their undertakings to a successful issue, they were always
able to weather the storm without being
swamped, the "uses of adversity" only stimu-
lating them to greater displays of energy and
fortitude. The most trying crisis happened in
1847-48, when trade was unusually depressed.
Prices were very low and unremunerative,
and the amount of wages paid for the twelve
months was only £20,000, or about one-half
the amount so spent in each of the preceeding
years. The quantity of work turned out in
that disastrous year was proportionately small,
being limited to 4,500 tons. The depression
was, however, of short duration, and the firm
had, by Herculean exertions, got fairly through
this season of adversity, when they were en-
couraged to additional enterprise by the event
of 1850—the discovery of iron stone, with
which Mr. Vaughan's name is indissolubly connected. During their struggling days the firm
displayed a degree of intrepidity that is seldom
paralled even in the often romantic annals of
manufacturing firms. They were dismayed
by no restrictions or conditions, however
stringent. Work fell into their hands that
few other firms were bold enough to undertake, from its being so difficult of accomplish-
ment; and they seldom failed to carry out to
the letter the most rigorous specifications.

Respecting one large contract into which they entered with the Board of Ordnance in the year 1855, it was reported that it had been rescinded in consequence of the Cleveland iron not being of the peculiar quality necessary for the purposes of that department. But Bolckow and Vaughan were not the men to let such a tempting bait come to a rival firm if they could avoid it, and they executed the contract to the entire satisfaction of the Ordnance Board. Indeed, it was said by the *Mining Journal* of that day, that the iron produced by this firm from the oolitic ironstone was so ductile and workable that they could and did execute castings that few firms would be willing to undertake, such as water pipes 3 ft. diameter and 12 ft. 4½ in. long, D retorts, 18¼ ft. long, cast for the Great Central Gas Company, and the rolling of Barlow's rails, which, from their peculiar form and varying thickness from centre to edge, were considered the most difficult to manipulate of any then made. Barlow's rails have been made at the Middlesbrough works from 17 ft. to 20 ft. in length without a flaw. Between 1850 and 1855 the firm supplied large quantities of rails for the East Indies under very peculiar, stringent, and difficult specifications, and so certain were they of the quality of their productions that they guaranteed their rails for a certain period of time.

Among the more extensive contracts of their kind undertaken at the Middlesbrough works, we may mention that for supplying the whole of the pipes to the West Middlesex Water Company, 9 ft. 6 in. long, by 3 ft. diameter ; a like contract for the Southwark and Vauxhall Company, 12 ft. 4½ in. long by 3 ft. diameter; and a contract for the Grand Junction Company's pipes, 12 ft. 4½ in. long, by 33 in. diameter.

It should not be forgotten that the existence of salt at Middlesbrough was discovered by Messrs. Bolckow and Vaughan, in their attempt to bore for pure water during 1863 and 1864. This discovery may ultimately prove of nearly as much importance to the Cleveland district, as that of the iron stone. In consequence of the disposal of the property and business of the firm to the present company, the further prosecution of this discovery was stopped for some time. The Directors decided, however, a year or two ago, to sink to the salt rock, which was found to be about a hundred feet thick; and, although doubtless a very arduous undertaking, the salt being at a depth of more than a thousand feet below the surface, it is hoped that it will lead to a successful result, and thus enable this valuable article to be supplied to the numerous chemical manufactories on the Tyne and elsewhere in the north.

More privileged than his partner, Mr. Bolckow has been spared to enjoy, in health, comfort, and affluence, the ease and honour due to his active and useful life. So far as the actual management of the firm is concerned, his labours came to an end when the Limited Liability Company was formed. Since then, however, so far from giving himself up to a life of indolent retirement, he has exhibited an increased interest in the affairs of the district which is so much one of his own creation, and sought to supply its more pressing wants. He was appropriately selected as the first Mayor of Middlesbrough, on the incorporation of the borough in 1853; and two years later, on the 7th April, 1855, he was presented by the Corporation with a full-length portrait (which has since then hung in the Council Chamber), in recognition of his merits and services. For many years afterwards, he occupied a seat at the Council Board, and exerted himself to promote the welfare of the growing municipality. He was elected the first president of the Middlesbrough Chamber of Commerce, and up to the present time he continues a useful member of that body. From the first, he has been one of the most indefatigable members of the Tees Conservancy Board, which has done a great deal in the way of improving the navigation of that now important river. Formerly, indeed, the Tees, from Middlesbrough upwards, was a shallow and tortuous stream, that could only be navigated by vessels of a light draught of water, and then only under circumstances of difficulty and danger. In the North Riding Infirmary, and other local charitable institutions, Mr. Bolckow has taken a deep interest, having assisted in founding the most of them.

Middlesbrough is one of the four new boroughs on Tees-side created under schedule D of the Representation of the People Act, 1867. Having done much to procure this recognition of the importance of the town, Mr. Bolckow was appropriately selected to become its first parliamentary representative. From the moment that Middlesbrough's enfranchisement was secured, it was allowed, by common consent, and with scarcely a single dissentient voice, that he should be asked to accept this honour, the highest that his fellow-townsmen could confer ; and although his instinctive inclination to shrink from public notice, and take his place among the workers rather than the leaders of public progress, led him at first to decline the honour, he was afterwards so convinced of his being the free and spontaneous choice of the people, that he declared his readiness to go to the poll. But this was unnecessary, for there was not a shadow of opposition to his candidature, although in each of the other three new boroughs—Darlington,

Hartlepool, and Stockton—fierce and pro-
tracted contests took place. In order to
qualify himself for a seat in Parliament, Mr.
Bolckow had to obtain a special Act, removing
the disabilities under which he laboured as an
alien. This Act received the Royal assent on
the 29th May, 1868, and provided that
" William Henry Ferdinand Bolckow shall be
naturalised, and shall have, hold, and enjoy all
rights, privileges, and capacities whatsoever
that he would, could, or might have had, held,
or enjoyed if he had been born within the
United Kingdom and had been a natural-born
subject of her Majesty the Queen." Of his
conduct in Parliament we care not now to
speak, further than to say that he is regular
in his attendance in St. Stephen's, and exhibits
in the highest degree that greatest merit of a
Parliamentary representative — an earnest
desire, and the necessary capacity, to advance
the interests of his constituents. He has
always been true to his professions at the
time of his election, to support all measures
which in his opinion would be benefical to the
country at large, and promote civil and
religious liberty. With Marc Antony, he
may say " I am no orator ;" he is not even a
prototype of Single-speech Hamilton, for we
are not aware that he has yet tried to make
even one set speech in the House ; but he has
none the less acquired an influence, especially

in commercial circles, that makes him a valuable unit in the ranks of the Liberal party.

So far back as 1854, Mr. Bolckow had made up his mind to present Middlesbrough with a public park and recreation ground. The difficulty of obtaining a suitable site, however, prevented him from giving effect to his intention until, in 1866, he acquired the ground now forming the Albert Park, for the sum of £18,000, and laid it out at a further cost of about £10,000, so that the total value of the gift was about £30,000. In August, 1868, the Park was formally opened by H.R.H. Prince Arthur, who was Mr. Bolckow's guest for two days. A general holiday was observed on the occasion, and the town wore an air of jubilation such as it has never known since. He received the following letter from the Queen :—

Pension Wallis, Lucerne, August 17, 1868.

SIR,—The circumstances attending the reception of H.R.H. Prince Arthur at the opening of the park at Middlesbrough have been reported to the Queen, and Her Majesty has learnt with great satisfaction how strong a feeling of loyalty towards herself and the Royal Family was evinced on the occasion.

Prince Arthur expressed verbally the gratification he derived from the loyal and enthusiastic greeting which was accorded to him, but the Queen is unwilling to leave unnoticed the conspicuous share taken by you in receiving and entertaining His Royal Highness, and has commanded me to return to you Her Majesty's thanks for your magnificent hospitality.—I have the honour to be, Sir, your obedient, humble servant,

(Signed)   T. M. BIDDULPH.

H. W. F. Bolckow, Esq.

In the cause of education, both elementary and technical, Mr. Bolckow has worked with a willing heart and an anxious mind. His experience of the Continent, and especially of his native country, which has long had a better system of education than any other country in Europe, showed him that the English artisan was far from being up to the mark. Compared with the German workman, he stood at a disadvantage, and even the *ouvriers* of Belgium and France had a training that put him in the shade. Mr. Bolckow saw this to his sorrow, and felt it to his loss. He could not make his workmen amenable to reason and a just preception of their true interests so readily as he could have done had they been better educated. Ignorance is the most fertile source of prejudice and superstition ; and Mr. Bolckow, although uniformly living on terms of amity and concord with his men, often found that their obstinacy and disregard of common sense were obstructions both to his and their progress. He aimed at removing this. With the generation to which he himself belonged he could do little good. But he could go to the root of evil, and confer upon the children that which had been withheld from their fathers. Up till the year 1867, Middlesbrough was deplorably short of adequate school accommodation, and it was calculated that not more than a third of the children available for that purpose were under educational discipline. At a cost of some £7,000, Mr. Bolckow built schools capable of providing for 900 children. This provision went a long way towards fully meeting the requirements of the town. The discipline of the school is of such a character that children of all classes, grades, and habits are admitted. For these munificent gifts to the town, the Corporation of Middlesbrough resolved to present Mr. Bolckow with a public address, and this ceremony, which took place on the 31st October, 1868, was the occasion of a crowded gathering in the Town Hall. The address set forth that " Under divine Providence, successful in your undertakings beyond the lot of most, you remembered that wealth cannot be more nobly applied than in advancing the condition of those around. This town—a town to a considerable extent of your own creation, indeed—owes you much : the present generation for your last princely gift, and the future for the knowledge which the schools now in course of erection will afford." In his reply, Mr. Bolckow said: "It has long been my earnest wish to contribute to the physical and intellectual requirements of your rapidly-increasing population, and I am thankful that divine Providence has enabled me thus far to accomplish my long cherished intentions."

We cannot linger over many other interesting events in Mr. Bolckow's life ; but we must
not omit to mention that he is chairman of the
Middlesbrough Exchange Company, Limited,
and holds a large stake in the concern. On the
22nd November, 1866, he laid the foundation-
stone of the Royal Exchange,—one of the
most important marts of commerce in the
North of England. On that occasion he stated
that " it had always been his determination
for Middlesbrough to become the metropolis
of the Cleveland Iron Trade, and he had no
doubt that that result would be brought about
by the erection of this building."

In the general election of 1874, Mr.
Bolckow again announced himself a candidate
for the representation of Middlesbrough—
declaring his acceptance of the Liberal
programme as represented by Mr. Gladstone,
with whom he had generally acted. But he
was not destined on this, as on the former
occasion, to have a "walk over." He was
opposed first of all by Mr. John Kane, the
Secretary of the Amalgamated Ironworkers
Society, an advanced politician, holding the
principles of the Land and Labour Representation League ; and afterwards by Mr.
W. R. I. Hopkins, whose candidature was
altogether contingent on that of Mr. Kane,
as will be found stated elsewhere. Mr.
Hopkins is regarded as the leader of the " fit

though few" body of Conservatives in Middlesbrough, and he was asked to champion their interests in the general election of 1868. Wisely, however, he then refused to involve the borough in the expense and excitement of a contested election, when the result was a foregone conclusion; and it was only because the Liberal party were apparently divided that he adopted a different course in 1874. The result of the election proved, by the infallible test of the Ballot, that Mr. Bolckow's is a real popularity, and that the people of Middlesbrough have a high appreciation of his worth and work. The official state of the poll showed: Bolckow, 3,719; Kane, 1,541; Hopkins, 996. During the contest Mr. Bolckow addressed numerous public meetings, and it was generally observed that he displayed an intimate acquaintance with the leading questions of the day, and great felicity in discussing them.

Of Mr. Bolckow's personal qualities we might speak with less reservation, were we not sure that the subject of these remarks would rather have anything unsaid that savours of flattery and adulation. But after all, the most that can be said of any man, however good or gifted, is contained in that graceful remark used by Lord John Russell in speaking of " Old Pam," his counsellor and friend, " those who knew him best esteemed him most;" and this is true in an eminent degree of Mr. Bolckow. To those who enjoy his friendship he is free, hospitable, and unreserved; and to all classes and objects alike that make just claims upon his time and purse, he is generous without the least show of ostentation. For many years he has displayed much taste as a virtuoso. In his noble house at Marton there is quite a unique display of old French, Dutch, and Flemish curiosities, in addition to many rare books and pictures, collected chiefly by himself in London. In variety and excellency, his collection of pictures is not surpassed by any private collection in the country. Not only are great names represented on the walls, but for the most part the best samples of the best artists have been brought together; several of the pictures have been engraved and have become very popular.

The following are a few of the leading pictures, most of which possess an historic interest and are of great value :—" The subsiding of the Nile," "Rebecca and Eleazar" and "Rachael," by Goodall; " Cattle " and " The Ferry," by Rosa Bonheur ; " Ancient Tombs in the Rocks at Lycia" and " The Bay of Naples," by W. Muller ; " Spanish Ladies " and " The Fruitseller," by Jno. Phillip; "Grandmother" and " Roast Pig," by T. Webster; " Homeless" and " The Silken Gown," by Thomas Faed; "Both Puzzled," and

E

"The China Merchant," by Erskine Nicol;
three Venetian paintings by E. W. Cooke;
"Evening of St. Agnes," by Maclise; "Snow
Storm in Cumberland" and "Noon day's rest,"
by T. S. Cooper; "Braemar" (one of Sir E.
Landseer's largest and best works); "Highland Shepherd," by Ansdell; "The Ballad,"
by John Faed; "Harvest" and "The Hill-
side Farm," by Linnell, senior; three paintings by Clarkson Stanfield; "Driving Home
the Flock," by David Cox; "Meeting of the
Avon and Severn," by Patrick Naysmith;
"Walton Bridges," by Turner; "St. Peter's,
Rome," by D. Roberts; "Merry Making in
the Olden Time," by Frith; "The Sick
Child," by Sir D. Wilkie; "The Stirrup Cup"
and "The Sign Painter," by Meissonnier;
with equally important samples of Poole,
Troyon, Frere, Bisschop, Egg, Eastlake,
Calderon, Millais, Gerome, W. Collins, Herr-
ing, Sant, etc.; and a very large and wonderfully executed enamel, with portrait of
Clemence Esaure, by Lepec.

As an indication of the interest taken in
Cleveland and its foremost pioneer, it is worthy
of note that biographical sketches of Mr.
Bolckow, with an admirably executed portrait
in each case, have appeared in the *British
Workman*, the *Practical Magazine*, *Home
Words*, and other publications; and in a series
of articles on important collections, the
Athenæum included the noble gallery at
Marton Hall.

III.—JOHN VAUGHAN.

CANNING said of South America, when he acknowledged its independence, " I called a new world into existence." It was a proud boast, but one which John Vaughan—comparing great things with small—could have made with as much show of reason as the famous English statesman   There are few who do not allow his claim to take a foremost place in the ranks of our pioneers.   Having only a limited and imperfect education, he had yet an intelligent eye for opportunities, much native tact, and an unbounded capacity for work.   With these qualities, he was just the man

" To burst his birth's invidious bar,
    Breasting the blows of circumstance,
    To grasp the skirts of happy chance,
    And grapple with his evil star."

And he did so most effectually. Commencing life in what might well be called the humblest walks of social life, he worked his way up to the highest that a merchant or manufacturer can attain, and died a millionaire. And yet he did not strike a vein of gold, nor did he obtain possession of the philosopher's stone. His name is not associated with any inventions or processes such as those that have obtained for Neilson, Bessemer, and others, a colossal fortune and a niche in the Temple of Fame. He sought not to win his spurs in any or either of the usual fields of distinction— literature, science, or art. He had great —even commanding—talent, and by turning it with marvellous aptitude to account, and making the most of it, he has left behind him a name that will not readily perish. The eternal glory of the man is, that he achieved for himself and others, by average resources, that which men of better opportunities could never have established. Let us be just, while we are also generous, to his pleasant memory. It was by hard work, tact, and foresight—not by mere luck or chance—that he was able to build up his colossal fortune. All the more credit, therefore, to himself; all the more hope and encouragement to others.

John Vaughan was born in the cathedral city of Worcester, on St. Thomas's Day, 1799. His father was an ironworker, who depended upon his daily toil for the support of his family. The most we know of him is that he was a man of considerable skill in his business, and of more than ordinary decision of character. His family were brought up in a respectable manner, and had the advantage of a good example. John was early taught that

" Man's but a sodger,
And life's but a fecht."

As a boy he worked in a scrap mill; as a
man he occupied more remunerative and
arduous positions—such as that of a roller.
But at an early age he practically proved that
" the child is father to the man." His plodding
disposition and inquiring habit of mind, led him
while still in his " teens " to take the highest
position as a workman, and earn better wages
than his neighbours. He graduated in one of
the best schools in the kingdom—the great
Dowlais works in South Wales—where he had
every possible facility for making himself
familiar with all the phases and ramifications
of the iron trade. Probably there were few
men who had at that time such an exhaustive
knowledge of the practice of iron-making.
Nor was he long of turning his attainments to good account. As "a prophet hath
not honour in his own country," he did not
succeed in obtaining at Dowlais the promotion
he aspired after, and he quitted that establishment, about the year 1825, to undertake managerial functions at a small ironworks at
Carlisle. Here he became acquainted with
and married his first wife. His next appointment was that of manager of the Walker
Ironworks, near Newcastle-on-Tyne, which
were established about the year 1832, by
Messrs. Losh, Wilson and Bell. Originally

the Walker Ironworks consisted of only one furnace, and it is a somewhat significant fact that this furnace was the first specially built for the use of Cleveland ironstone, which was obtained from mines near Whitby, belonging to a Mrs. Clark. John Vaughan, however, could not have been in any way directly concerned with this circumstance; for three years previously he had joined Mr. Bolckow in starting the Middlesbrough works. From this point there is so much unity in the lives of the two partners that they are almost inseparable. For a number of years they were nearly as much part and parcel of each other as the Siamese twins. They had one object —or objects—in common; they lived, not together, but next door to each other; they were continually in each other's company, consulting, controlling, planning, advising, for the same ends. But it is necessary to make a distinction somewhere between two men who, however identical in their lives, had each his own individuality; and for the sake of continuity, we shall here proceed to carry our narrative up to the point of Mr. Vaughan's lamented decease.

It was Mr. Vaughan who fixed upon Middlesbrough as the site of the new enterprise which he and his partner resolved to undertake about the close of the year 1839. Being the practical man of the firm, this matter was

left entirely in his hands. We are not aware
of the precise reasons which actuated his
choice. Did he dream of the treasures which
these hills contained ? Or did the near proximity to coal and shipping facilities offer
inducements ? Or had he formed a hypothesis
of his own—and this seems from the course
taken by subsequent events to be the more
likely surmise—as to the nodules of ironstone,
which the disintegrating effects of the weather,
left exposed on the bold bluff coast between
Whitby and Saltburn ? Here at any rate the
firm launched, perchance with "fear and
trembling," their little venture, which was
originally constructed on a very modest scale,
and included only the manufacture of finished
iron and its conversion into different kinds of
machinery. The Middlesbrough of that day
was a village of some 4,600 or 4,800 inhabitants. It had two sources of trade—the
shipment of coal, and a small pottery ; but no
ironworks had as yet been built from one end
of Cleveland to the other. As one of the
Middlesbrough owners, from whom the new
firm acquired their site, Joseph Pease, the
first Quaker member of Parliament, was one
of the first to become acquainted with Mr.
Vaughan, and at the request of the latter he
gave the firm an introduction to several colliery owners, in South Durham, couched in
the following terms :—

2nd day, 12th month, 1841.

The bearer, Mr. John Vaughan, of the firm of Bolckow and Vaughan, being about to visit the owners of coal, wishes me to recommend him as likely to become an extensive consumer.

(Signed)   JOSEPH PEASE.

As coal was at that time rather a drug in the market, Mr. Vaughan would probably get a welcome reception from the coal owners, despite the curt, cautious, and not over friendly note of introduction written by his patron. Like all new firms, Messrs. Bolckow and Vaughan, in commencing, had many difficulties to encounter, and these were not of merely temporary duration, but lasted over a period of at least eight or ten years, during which Mr. Vaughan appeared to be proof against fatigue and empowered with ubiquity. He threw his whole soul into the success and aggrandisement of the firm, and the operation of his practical experience soon gained it a name for the excellent quality of the work produced. We learn from a local history, that "Messrs. Bolckow and Vaughan made the engines in 1843 of the steamer English Rose, the first steamboat built in the port of Stockton." Mr. J. W. Ord, three years later, writes in his history of Cleveland, that " in the ironworks belonging to Bolckow and Vaughan, not only are all sorts of cast and wrought iron executed, but rolling mills are in operation for the production of bar iron and rails of every description."

On the 14th day of February, 1846, the firm commenced the manufacture of pig iron, having erected four blast furnaces at Witton Park, near Bishop Auckland, for that purpose. There were then no blast furnaces nearer than Consett and Tow Law, and as the railway facilities of the place had only been imperfectly developed, the firm had often considerable difficulties in obtaining the supplies of pig iron and fuel necessary for their works. These had by this time attained a considerable bulk—the quantity of iron used in 1846 being 20,000 tons, while the consumption of coal was 100,000 tons. Mr. I. L. Bell assigns as the reason that induced the selection of Witton Park as site for the new works, the fact that the firm had an offer of a supply of ironstone from the coal-fields near Bishop Auckland; but, as had happened to their colleagues on the Tyne years before, in these expectations they were disappointed, and were therefore compelled, like them, to have recourse to the use of the Whitby ironstone. It may be interesting to state, that when Messrs. Bolckow and Vaughan built the Witton Park furnaces, there were only other ten works of the same class in the North of England. The following table shows their particulars :—

Name of Works.	Date of Erection.	No. of Furnaces.
Lemington	1800	2
Birtley	1827	3
Ridsdale	1835	2
Hareshaw	1836	3
Wylam	1836	1
Consett	1840	7
Walker	1843	1
Stanhope	1845	1
Crook Hall	1845	7
Tow Law	1845-6	5
Total		32

And now we come to what is in many respects the most interesting epoch in the career of Mr. Vaughan—his connection with the discovery of the Cleveland ironstone. Many erroneous versions of this matter have been published. It is popularly supposed, indeed, that the very existence of ironstone in the Cleveland hills was unknown until Mr. Vaughan stumbled upon it. The most commonly accepted, although a most erroneous explanation of the discovery, is that which represents Mr. Vaughan as having quite accidentally and unintentionally stumbled upon a nodule of ironstone while out shooting. There are few fallacies that have not a basis in fact, and this one is no exception to the rule. But in order that Mr. Vaughan's real connection with this discovery may be clearly defined, it is necessary to take a retrospective glance at the ante-iron era in Middlesbrough.

A great antiquity has been assigned to the
actual discovery of the Cleveland ironstone.
In his illustrations of the geology of Cleveland, published in 1829, Professor Phillips
says that "ironstone abounds on this coast,"
and he speaks of ironworks that were established by the Monks near Rievaulx Abbey,
in Bilsdale, and in the valley of Hackness.
Again, in his "History and Antiquities of
Cleveland," published in 1846, Mr. J. W.
Ord says that "Bransdale, Rosedale, and
probably some of the other dales, contain
quantities of ironstone, although at present in
disuse." He adds, "The vast heaps of iron
slag, and numerous remains of ancient works,
prove that much iron must formerly have
been produced there." On the strength of
these and other collateral criteria, it has been
argued that the Romans on the one hand, and
the Monks on the other, were aware of the
existence of ironstone in the Cleveland hills,
and worked it at a very early period. From
this view, however, Mr. John Marley, of Darlington, a mining engineer of eminence, em-
phatically dissents, thinking it very question-
able "whether the Romans or the Monks
ever smelted any part of the main bed of
ironstone, which has in recent years proved
such a source of wealth to the North, because
in the various remains of slag and refuse left
by them in Bilsdale, Bransdale, Rosedale,

Furnace House in Fryupdale, Rievaulx Abbey, and other places, no traces of the main seam of ironstone have been found, although 'dogger band ' (or thin clay · bands of ironstone) and 'nodules' have been so found along with the charcoal and slag."

Coming down to more recent times, however, we are confronted by the most unequivocal testimony that the knowledge of the mineral wealth of Cleveland is much older than is commonly supposed. In 1811, the late William W. Jackson, of Normanby Hall, had samples of ironstone from his property, near Upsal, sent to the Lemington Ironworks on the Tyne, for the purpose of being tested. The result was not encouraging. "Tell your master," was the reply, "that it is good for nothing." From this time forward, numerous attempts were made to win the Cleveland ironstone to practical account, but failure seems to have attended nearly every effort in this direction. Its value was not understood. One writer says, in 1828, "It has been ascertained to yield 15 per cent. of iron." This is not above one-half the average percentage obtained at the present time. Again we find that on the 18th day of May, 1836, a cargo of fifty-five tons of ironstone was sent from Grosmont to Whitby, and from thence shipped to the Birtley Ironworks, near Newcastle, by the Whitby Stone Company, which was formed for the purpose of developing traffic, including freestone, whinstone, and ironstone, for the Whitby and Pickering Railway. The experiment was attended with doubtful results, but it did not deter the company from sending a second quantity to the Tyne Iron Company, who, after putting it to the test, returned the cheering intimation that " they were ashamed to see such refuse on the quay!" The next experiment of which we have any record was made by the Devon Iron Company, now defunct, who had blast furnaces at Alloa, near Stirling. It was through Mr. D. Neasham, of the late firm of Neasham and Company, of the Portrack Lane Ironworks, Stockton, that a cargo of ironstone obtained near Coatham was sent to the Devon Company. That gentleman received a letter in reply to the effect that there was no iron in the stone; that it was not even worth trying; and that he should give himself no further trouble about it. When Mr. J. W. Ord published his work on Cleveland in 1846, he declared the ironstone to be " at present of little value except as ballast, and scarcely of sufficient importance to encourage speculation."

It is unnecessary to follow the progress of the various efforts to make the Cleveland ironstone a marketable commodity, for they all began and ended with doubt, difficulty, and discouragement. We have said enough

to show that as a commercial product the ironstone was discredited and condemned. Until
Messrs. Bolckow and Vaughan came upon the
field, its application to the purposes of iron
manufacture was regarded as all but impracticable—so much so, indeed, that when the
latter proposed to enter into leases for its
developement on the estate of Mr. E. W.
Jackson, at Eston, that gentleman said he
would not " assist to ruin Messrs. Bolckow and
Vaughan and spoil the estate." But the time
came and the man; in what manner we shall
see.

It was in 1846, as already stated, that
Messrs. Bolckow and Vaughan established
their works at Witton Park. The *localé* was
admirably chosen in respect of commanding
easy and near access to the coal and carboniferous lime-stone measures, as well as to the
" vein " or " rider " stone from Teesdale and
Weardale. But their supplies of ironstone
at the best were irregular and precarious, and
they were continually on the alert for more
reliable and trustworthy sources. In pursuance of this aim, they procured some
thousands of tons off the coast between Redcar
and Skinningrove in the spring of 1848, and
having shipped it to Middlesbrough they conveyed it thence per railway to Witton Park.
This is believed to have been the first practical application of the discovery of the main

seam in the north of the Cleveland measures.
On the 7th August, 1848, Messrs. Bolckow
and Vaughan made arrangements with Mr. A.
L. Maynard, one of the lessors of the ironstone at Skinningrove, for a supply of ironstone from that district. It is said that before Mr. Vaughan had issued instructions as
to how this ironstone was to be treated, the
furnace manager emptied the first few
wagons of stone into the refuse heap, as
"freestone stuff," although we have heard the
statement contradicted. In 1849 the Skinningrove mines came into the hands of
Messrs. Bolckow and Vaughan, and were
worked by them until October of the following
year, when they were transferred to Messrs.
Losh, Wilson, and Bell, of the Walker Ironworks. All the energies of Mr. Vaughan
were strained at the time to obtain a cheap,
ample, and convenient supply of ironstone.
Although the furnace manager reported un-
favourably on the first cargo sent from
Skinningrove, Mr. Vaughan soon saw for
himself that it was greatly superior in yield
to the Whitby ironstone, which the firm had
previously used to a large extent. Under
his auspices, therefore, trial drifts were made
in the Upleatham Hills, at Eston, and at
Normanby, with a view to the further development of the mineral; but the "top
seam," which is the most irregular, both in

thickness and in quality, was the only one then discovered. Although thus disappointed, Mr. Vaughan was neither disheartened nor dismayed. He continued his examination of the Cleveland Hills until, on the 8th day of June, 1850, he stumbled upon the main seam of ironstone. He made this discovery in company with Mr. John Marley, mining engineer of Darlington, whose account of the incident it may be well to quote here. Mr. Marley says:—" Mr. Vaughan and myself, having gone to examine the hills for the most suitable place for boring, we decided to ascend to the east, adjoining Sir J. H. Lowther's grounds, and so walk along to Lady Hewley's grounds on the west. In ascending the hill in Mr. C. Dryden's grounds, we picked up two or three small pieces of ironstone. We, therefore, continued our ascent until we came to a quarry hole, from whence this ironstone had been taken for roads, and next, on entering Sir J. H. Lowther's grounds to the west, a solid rock of ironstone was lying bare, up-wards of sixteen feet thick. I need scarcely say that, having once found this bed, we had no difficulty in following the outcrop in going westward, without any boring, as the rabbit and fox holes therein were plentiful as we went. We also examined the place in Lackenby Banks, squared down in 1811 or 1812 by the late Mr. Thomas Jackson, of

Lackenby. The period from the 8th June, 1850, till the middle of August following was occupied in completing arrangements for opening out this ironstone, and the first trial quarry was begun on the 13th of August, 1850. A temporary tramway was soon laid down, and by the 2nd of September, 1850, the first lot of seven tons was brought down in small tubs to the highway side, from thence carted to Cargo Fleet, and thence again by rail to Witton Park Ironworks, being about three weeks after actually seeing the ironstone, and by this method 4,041 tons were sent away by the 28th December following."

Such is Mr. Marley's plain and simple narrative of a discovery that has led to such splendid results. The extent and value of the Cleveland ironstone having been approximately ascertained, Mr. Vaughan made haste to conclude leases for the working of large royalties at Eston, and as the lessors regarded it as only a doubtful thing at the best, the firm were enabled to do this on the most advantageous terms. It is said that Mr. Vaughan, in making his lease, kept all knowledge of his discovery from the owners of the land, or, at any rate, hinted at the ironstone as being problematical in its extent and suitability. At all events, their royalty payment was not more than fourpence per ton, whereas of late years it has averaged

F

sixpence, and is, in some cases, as much as ninepence per ton of 20 cwt.

Of the subsequent operations of Messrs. Bolckow and Vaughan, as a firm, we have left ourselves so little room to speak here that we must refer them to our sketch of Mr. Bolckow, and this may be done with all the more appropriateness, seeing that in later years the latter exercised more control over the concern than his partner's failing health could allow him to do. We cannot, however, do justice to Mr. Vaughan without speaking of his excellent personal qualities, of his amiability in domestic life, of his generosity, his equable and benevolent disposition, and his keen and active sympathy with the interests and instincts of his workmen. No man was more familiar than he with

"The short but simple annals of the poor,"

and no one was more ready to extend a helping hand to a case of real distress, or to recognise and reward merit in those under him. One who knew him well has said that "a foul word, or an angry hasty word, never escaped his lips; not that he did not become excited and vexed when aught went wrong in the works—never being satisfied until he himself had put it right, matterless the personal labour or time employed—and all the men not only felt his earnestness and power, but tacitly acknowledged their mistakes and

made amends for the future. Such a master
created good and faithful servants. Among
the lower class, he was singularly looked up
to, yet not servily. Without the slightest
presumption on his wealth, or the least
affectation of superiority, he was sincerely
respected by all grades, and acquitted himself well in each." When he died, Mr.
Vaughan bequeathed to his only son, Mr.
Thomas Vaughan, personal property representing about half a million sterling, to his widow
he left £3,000 a-year for life, and to her
off-spring by her two former marriages no
less an amount than £130,000 ;—besides
the estate and mansion of Gunnergate, with
its extensive pleasure grounds and gardens,
Cleveland Lodge, and other property. He died
in his sixty-ninth year, on Wednesday, September 16, 1868. Having fought a good fight,
he finished his course in the presence of his
son, Mr. Thomas Vaughan, and other sorrow-
ing members of his family.

"God's finger touched him, and he slept !"

Tranquilly and happily he passed away, after
a long life bordering on the "allotted span,"
crowded with toil and vicissitude, and crowned
with a measure of success which falls to the
lot of few men.

IV.—ISAAC WILSON

Mr. Isaac Wilson is justly entitled to take a front place in the ranks of the pioneers of the Cleveland iron trade. When he came to Middlesbrough in 1841, it was not the "waste and howling wilderness" that Joseph Pease and those who were concerned with him in the purchase of the Middlesbrough Estate had found it twenty years before. But it was in all respects an uninviting, crude, and needy town—uninviting, because it was situated almost in the centre of a huge marsh, and was considered anything but healthy; crude, because it was in a half-formed, angular, and transition state; and needy, because, like all newly created communities, its municipal, religious, and educational requirements yet remained to be provided for to a great extent. Mr. Wilson has assisted, more than most of those whose fortunes have been identified with the place, to tone down all rhomboids, odd points, and angles, to foster its industrial capacities, and to lay the foun-

dations of its present and prospective success.
Born at Kendal, in February, 1822, Mr.
Wilson is the scion of an old and highly respectable Westmoreland family. He can trace
his descent in a direct line back to the time
of Anthony Wilson, of Little Langdale, in
the parish of Grasmere, who died in 1639.
His father Isaac Wilson —son of John and
Sarah Wilson, of Kendal—was born in 1784,
and died at Kendal in 1844. His mother was
the daughter of John Jowitt, of Leeds, whose
family has been well known and highly respected in that town for many generations.
Mr. Wilson's father followed the trade of a
woollen manufacturer in the picturesque
little town of Kendal, but as the Lake district
is more famed for its scenic beauties and in-
vigorating breezes than for its industrial
prestige, we are not surprised to find that the
manufacturing operations carried on at that
time were on a somewhat restricted scale.
Accordingly, it behoved the subject of this
sketch to look out, when he had attained mature years, for a larger and more promising
field of operations.

Circumstances brought Mr. Wilson into
intimate contact with the Messrs. Pease, of
Darlington—to whom he was related—about
the year 1841. The late Mr. Joseph Pease,
with that eagerness to help forward deserving
young men that always characterised him,

took an interest in his young relative, and proposed to him to settle down at Middlesbrough. Coming events were then "casting their shadows before" so clearly, that Mr. Pease looked forward to a great future for Middlesbrough. He pointed out to Mr. Wilson that there was an excellent opening for the erection of works at that town, as it was so near the Durham coal-field and the principal harbours on the north-east coast, in addition to possessing railway facilities that were considered at that time of day exceptionally good. Mr. Wilson came to Middlesbrough on these representations, and, through Mr. Pease, he became intimate with Mr. Richard Otley, who will be remembered as the first secretary of the Stockton and Darlington Railway—an office which he held for many years. It so happened that Mr. Otley had then engaged in the business of an earthenware manufacturer, along with the late Mr. Davison. Mr. Wilson was asked to join the venture. He gave his ready consent, and for several years his attention was almost exclusively bestowed on this business. It is worthy of note, that the Pottery was then the only industrial establishment in the town, except the works of Bolckow and Vaughan, and another small engineering works. To the west of the pottery, which is situated between the Ferry Landing and the Docks, within two hundred

yards of the river, there was nothing but a
few coal-heavers' dwellings, and on every
other side the country was either marshy or
agricultural land. Even at this comparatively
recent date, the pilgrim fathers of Middlesbrough were accustomed to shoot snipe and
other aquatic fowl, within a hundred yards of
the site of the Pottery, while the district
known as the Marshes, where there is now
quite a congeries of works of different kinds,
and where smoke and flame are belched forth
from a thousand chimneys, was so "truly
rural," that the early settlers used it for re-
creative purposes. It is not necessary to be
an old man to remember the time when the
whole stretch of ground between Gosford
Street and Newport exhibited no trace of industrial life. Now, it is hardly possible to
find anything like the same amount of activity,
within a similarly circumscribed area, even
in the largest centres of British industry.
To adapt the marsh land on the west side of
the borough for the construction of works, it
was covered with slag obtained from the blast
furnaces, that had meanwhile been started in
the district, thus giving a solid and sure foundation, and converting this waste product into
a highly useful commodity.

But we are anticipating somewhat the
proper sequence of our narrative. Mr. Wilson
had not long been connected with the Pottery,

when he and his partners erected ironworks
of limited extent on a piece of ground
immediately adjoining their earthenware
works. The development of this venture
was never followed out, and in 1844, Mr.
Wilson, who had meanwhile formed an in-
timacy with Mr. Edgar Gilkes, joined with
him in the partnership which resulted in the
establishment of the Tees Engine Works.
Under the style of Gilkes, Wilson, and Company these works were carried on until 1865,
when they were merged in the concern that
has since borne the name of Hopkins, Gilkes
and Company. Mr. Wilson has been chairman
since the commencement. The operations
of the company have all along embraced the
manufacture of crude iron, and the production
of plates, rails, bar and angle iron, and railway
chairs of every specification. But besides
being one of the largest, it has also been one
of the most prosperous concerns in Cleveland
for a number of years.

In the year 1853, blast furnaces were built
at Cargo Fleet, below Middlesbrough, by the
firm of Gilkes, Wilson, Leatham and Company.
Of this large concern—the largest of its kind
in the Middlesbrough district, at that time
—with the exception of Bolckow, Vaughan,
and Company. In this concern (which was
the second set of furnaces erected in the
district), Mr. Wilson was a partner. It was

his first introduction to the manufacture of
crude iron. In 1858, Mr. Leatham, who was
a brother of the present member for Hud-
dersfield, and a son-in-law of Mr. Joseph
Pease, of Darlington, was removed by death,
and his place in the firm was supplied by
Mr. J. B. Pease (since deceased), the son-in-
law of Mr. Wilson. The style of the firm was
now altered to that of Gilkes, Wilson, Pease,
and Company, and the works are still carried
on under that designation.

Immediately adjacent to the Tees-side
ironworks, there are the Linthorpe works,
with six large blast furnaces, carried on by
the firm of Lloyd and Company. In this
undertaking Mr. Wilson is largely interested,
and was one of its original promoters. Mr.
Lloyd, whose name gives its style to the firm,
came originally to the Cleveland district to
fill a responsible position in the National
Provincial Bank at Stockton, and through
Mr. Thomas Snowdon, whose daughter he
espoused, he became connected with the iron
trade.

The bent of Mr. Wilson's mind is so constituted that he cannot stand listlessly by
while public business—no matter how thank-
less, difficult, and unremunerative—remains
to be attended to. From first to last, we
should say, that a full third of his time has
been given up to public business, from which

he could not hope to obtain either honour or reward. He was one of the first commissioners that had the honour of being elected Mayor of the borough of Middlesbrough, and since the town was incorporated in 1853, he has sat continuously at the Council Board. His counsel is always listened to with deference and respect, and he never shirked his due share of the more onerous and unpleasant minutiæ of committee work.

It is to the interests of the Tees navigation that Mr. Wilson has contributed his most zealous and valuable services. What Sir Joseph Cowen has been to the Tyne, Mr. Wilson has been to the Tees. He was one of the original members of the Conservancy Commission when it was constituted by the Act of 1852, and has for many years held the office of chairman. Through evil and through good report he has struggled to promote the ends for which the commission was formed. It was a difficult, and not unfrequently a dismal, task, for the obstacles to be surmounted were almost appalling, and the resources at the disposal of the Commissioners were very limited.

The position of affairs in the early history of the commission required the utmost tact and discrimination, and it is worthy of note, that Mr. Wilson was able to maintain the good opinion of all parties at a time when

party feeling occasionally ran very high.
But he showed in this, as in all other matters
to which he put his hands, that he possessed
those qualifications in an eminent degree, and
his judicious conduct at the helm enabled the
somewhat unmixible elements of which the
Commission was composed to operate for the
timely and judicious development of the trade
of the district. Still continuing to preside
over the Conservancy of the river, Mr. Wilson
has lived to reap some satisfaction for his
pains, for the Tees is now in a fair way
of realising the end of all his hopes and
efforts.

We have already indicated the interest that
Mr. Joseph Pease manifested in his young
Kendal protege. That interest was never
allowed to flag, until Mr. Pease had the satisfaction of seeing Mr. Wilson serving on the
Board of Directors of the Stockton and Darlington Railway. His administrative capacity
was so conspicuously exhibited, while he
occupied this position, that when the sectional
management was merged in that of the
Central Board, Mr. Wilson was unanimously
appointed a director of the North-Eastern
Railway. His long experience, and close
attention to financial and engineering details,
have made him quite an authority on the
difficult and comprehensive art of railway

management, and probably there are none of
his co-directors whose opinions carry greater
weight.

Mr. Wilson has always taken an active part
in political affairs—always on the Liberal
side. His popularity in his adopted town
was so well established that when Middlesbrough became a Parliamentary borough in
1867, he was at once mentioned as one who
had great claims to be elected the first
member. A large and influential deputation,
composed from nearly every class in the
constituency, waited upon him for this purpose, and presented a requisition signed by
considerably over 2,000 electors. But he
hesitated, probably as much as Donna Inez did
in an even more delicate situation; and when
it was announced that Mr. Bolckow had agreed
to go to the poll, Mr. Wilson at once chival-
rously yielded up the preference to what he
no doubt regarded as the now sitting member's
superior claims. The old Greek stoic said,
"If I were not Diogens, I would be Alex-
ander." If the electors of Middlesbrough
had not had the choice of Mr. Bolckow, they
would undoubtedly have accepted Mr. Wilson
as their representative. At the General
Election of 1874, he acted as chairman of Mr.
Bolckow's committee, and won golden opinions
for the firmness, dignity, and moderation with

which he conducted a contest in which strong feeling was roused and great principles were at stake.

In the year 1847, Mr. Wilson married Anna Dorothy, daughter of Robert Benson, Esq., of Parkside, Kendal, by whom he has had one son and five daughters.

V. —JOSEPH DODDS, M.P.

THOSE who know of Mr. Joseph Dodds in his professional capacity alone may be inclined to wonder at finding his name at the head of this article. But it is not always the men who are put most prominently forward, that are chiefly entitled to prominence. The most indefatigable workers often keep their identity in the background. In commerce, as in politics, and other relations of life, there are often wheels within wheels—*an imperium in imperio.* Thus it is in the case of Mr. Joseph Dodds. Professionally a solicitor, in the enjoyment of a practice probably second in value and importance to none in the North of England, he is, at the same time, a large ironmaster, and a recognised representative of the industrial interests in the House of Commons. On these grounds he is fairly entitled to take his place among the Pioneers of the Cleveland Iron Trade. But when we have said this, we have not said all. The prosperity of a community depends not so much upon the initiation of great projects as upon their successful consummation; and it is almost a trite reflection that a condition of mere animalism, in which all the grosser attributes of humanity are rampant, is not the state most conducive to permanent and properly-directed success; nor is it possible for a new community, like that of Middlesbrough or Stockton, to overtake all their requirements in anything like the ratio in which they arise unless governed by men of zeal, faith, enterprise, and foresight. Such a man is Joseph Dodds. He found Cleveland—that is the wide and important district embraced in that name—in an infantile condition. It required care, nutriment, and constant attention. Although undoubtedly an infant Hercules, it might have broken down or run to seed under other treatment. As it is, it has had all the advantages that both natural and artificial gifts could bestow. No sooner did an urgent want arise than it was promptly met, and generally to the fullest extent. Joseph Dodds was in all the counsels of the men who had this onerous work on hand. Advising, planning, and suggesting, he is the head and front of many improvements and enterprises that where fathered on others. Probably, there is no great scheme affecting the material progress of the district, that has not had the benefit of his assistance and co-operation in

one form or another. While fighting, like
Hal o' the Wynd "for his ain hand," he has
also striven earnestly, laboriously, and consci-
entiously to promote the general weal of those
by whom he was surrounded. His untiring
exertions have met their reward in the attainment of a position of affluence, influence,
honour and respect,

Born on the 10th October, 1819, Mr. Joseph
Dodds is now in the fifty-fifth year of his
age. His father, a farmer near Winston, a
village on the banks of the Tees not far from
Barnard Castle, is still living, and a hale
active man, although over 90 years of age.
After receiving his early training at a
dame's school in his native village, he was
sent to the parish school of Winston, and from
thence he was transferred to the Gainford
Academy, then under the charge of the late
Rev. W. Bowman, M.A. Under this able preceptor he made rapid and distinguished progress, carrying off many academic honours,
and excelling particularly in the classics.
Leaving Gainford Academy on attaining his
seventeenth year, he commenced his business
career in the office of the late Mr. Thomas
Bowes, of Darlington, from whence he removed to Barnard Castle, to take a situation
under the late Mr. Weldon of that town.
About 1841, he removed to Stockton, at the
request of his relative, the late Mr. Matthew

Bowser, land agent, Thornaby Grange, who had thrown out inducements as to his kinsman's ultimate succession to the business. Simultaneously with his employment by Mr. Bowser, young Dodds assisted in the office of Messrs. Bayley and Newby, solicitors, Stockton; and in 1846, he was articled to Mr. Bayley, on the understanding that he would ultimately be admitted into partnership with that gentleman. But the death of Mr. Bayley put a period to this prospect; and Mr. Dodds, after qualifying for the position of an attorney and solicitor, commenced practice on his own account, having acquired the connection that belonged to his late master.

It will thus be seen that it was not until 1851 that Mr. Dodds had actually established himself in his profession; and his connection being limited, his prospects did not point in the direction of rapid or great prosperity. But his was a character, formed by nature, to overcome opposition and impress its sign manual on the community in which he lived. The first official position he held in his adopted town was that of a committeeman, and afterwards honorary secretary of the Stockton Mechanics' Institution, of which, for many years past he has been, and still is, vice-president. In 1852 he was elected a member of the Town Council. He was then only 33 years of age—a time of life when few men can command the weight and influence necessary to secure their election to civic honours. In 1857 he was elected Mayor of the borough, in preference to the late Mr. William Turnbull, shipbuilder, who was also put in nomination. On the expiry of his year of office as Mayor, he was again elected a member of the Council, and he has since continued, with only one short interval, to retain his seat at the Council board, being still an alderman of the borough.

On the motion of his friend and client, Mr. H. W. F. Bolckow, M.P., Mr. Dodds was unanimously elected chief clerk to the Tees Conservancy Commissioners, in succession to the late Mr. J. Radcliffe Wilson, town clerk of Stockton. This was in 1858. The first business undertaken by Mr. Dodds, as chief clerk to the Tees Conservancy Commissioners, was to solicit through Parliament the Tees Conservancy Act, 1858. This Act is, in one respect, unique. It confers upon the Commissioners powers which, as yet have not been conferred upon any other public body exercising similar functions,—to reclaim, with the sanction of the Board of Trade, portions of the foreshore of the Tees, the proceeds arising from the sale of which are divided between the Queen as owner of the foreshore, the frontager, and the Tees Conservancy Commissioners in the proportion of one-fourth to each of the former, and two-fourths to the Commissioners.

Under these powers, originally, we believe, suggested by William Fallows, Esq., of Middlesbrough, and obtained mainly through his indefatigable exertions, upwards of 1,000 acres of valuable land have already been reclaimed from the bed of the river, the sale of which has, or will realise to the Commissioners, upwards of £75,000. Further large tracts of land are now, or shortly will be, in course of reclamation, with the combined result of improving the navigation, and materially augmenting the resources of the Commissioners. The services of Mr. Dodds in obtaining from Parliament these novel and valuable powers, received the special recognition of the Commissioners. The Tees Conservancy Commission was not then in the prosperous position it has since attained. Originally formed in 1852, this body found themselves hampered, on their foundation, with a debt of something like £80,000, that had been incurred by their predecessors, the old Tees Navigation Company. This was such a dead weight about their necks, that they were unable to undertake any important schemes for the improvement of the river until three years afterwards. Even then the revenue of the Commission was little more than £4,000 per annum, so that it seemed in-

sufficient to justify the outlay of a large expenditure. But without paralysing their progress by further pecuniary embarrassments,
they instituted a graduated system of improvements, which has now made the Tees one
of the most important highways in the North,
second only to the Tyne. The annual revenue
of the Commissioners is now upwards of
£23,000, being an increase within twenty
years of about 600 per cent. The value of
the trade of the Tees ports has increased in
a corresponding, if not greater ratio. In
1864, the value of the goods exported from
Stockton was only £5,136; last year it was
£14,989. The exports of Middlesbrough in
1864 were only estimated at £390,650; last
year they reached the enormous sum of
£2,647,883! Within the same period the
trade of the Hartlepools has also considerably
increased, although to a comparatively inconsiderable extent—the value of the exports for
1864 being £2,161,600 as compared with
£2,271,492. The only port on the north-
east coast that can at all compáre with Middlesbrough as regards the development of
the export trade, is Newcastle; the value of
the exports of the latter town having increased from £978,472 in 1864 to £3,055,357
in 1872! It is to the improvement of the
Tyne navigation in the one case, and to that
of the Tees in the other, that the enormous

increase of the shipping trade of both these ports is chiefly due. Having so far vindicated the importance of this phase of Mr. Dodds' career, we may be permitted to dwell upon it at still greater length.

When the Tees Conservancy Act of 1852 was obtained, no means had been taken to improve the river below Cargo Fleet. The sand banks were continually altering their position, and the stream was always divided into two and sometimes into three channels. The depth in the best water was often less than two feet, and it was generally very crooked and irregular. Great difficulty was experienced by even the smallest craft in navigating the channel, and the casualties to shipping were frequent. Under the old Tees Navigation Act, jetties had been constructed for the purpose of driving the channel over to the north; but these works were only constructed bit by bit, in order to get rid of temporary difficulties as they arose, and their effect was to damage the south channel without improving the north. The tonnage of the port of Middlesbrough was gradually getting worse instead of better. The diversion of the Port Clarence traffic to West Hartlepool on the opening of the docks at the latter place gave it a severe blow. Another cause of its decline was the limitation of the exports of coal, which, as blast furnaces were erected in the district, was used in the neighbourhood of Middlesbrough for smelting purposes. For the year ending October, 1855, the tonnage of the port did not exceed 290,658 tons. This was lower than the annual tonnage of the port for the previous twenty years.

It was under these depressing circumstances that the Tees Conservancy Commissioners commenced work. They first directed themselves to shutting up the north and middle channels, thus guiding the whole of the tidal water through the south channel. Through the Cargo Fleet shoal, which had been a great obstruction to the navigation of the river, a channel was cut 200 feet in breadth, and with a depth of seven feet at low water. About fifteen miles of training walls were erected. Dredging operations were commenced and carried on uninterruptedly. Matters were so far mended that the only important remaining barrier to the safe and easy navigation of the river was the state of the bar. But herein lay a terrible source of danger. For two miles westward of the bar, the sea broke during storms on either side of the channel, and from the overlapping of the gare, strangers were unable to detect any smooth water through which to navigate their vessels in safety. To obviate this peril, the Commissioners commenced the erection of a breakwater, which is still in progress, and in the construction of which over 3,000,000 tons of slag will be used! The effect of this and other improvements, will be to shut up the lateral channels in which the flowing and ebbing tides waste their strength, to enclose the shifting sand banks within permanent walls, to confine the scouring power to the proper channel, to shelter effectually the lower reaches of the river, and to enlarge the area of the anchoring pools. The depth of water at the bar, which in 1858 was only four feet and now seldom exceeds nine, will be at least 14 feet at low water, and the entrance to the channel will be marked by beacons between which vessels may be run with confidence and safety.

Up to the present time, the Commissioners have expended something like £250,000 in their improvements; but they have still gigantic schemes in hand or in contemplation, to carry out which they required borrowing powers for another £100,000. Of this sum £30,000 will be appropriated to the construction of a graving dock, hitherto a great want on the Tees. The rest will go to the completion of the breakwater, to blasting and removing the Eighth Buoy Scarp, which has narrowed the navigable channel to the extent of 100 to 200 feet, and to the completion of dredging operations necessary to secure a depth of 14 feet below Stockton Stone Bridge. When all these projects shall have passed from the region of speculation into that of fulfilment and fact, the Tees will have become second to no other river in the kingdom for all the purposes and requirements of navigation; and it may be expected to take the pre-eminent position, as a highway of commerce, to which its merits and achievements entitle it.

Mr. Dodds has been one of the principal advisers and promoters, of all these and other improvements of a collateral kind, that have taken place in the navigation of the Tees, since he became Chief Clerk to the Commission. His interest in the work was not confined to his official duties pure and simple. Outside their limits, he took an active part in "making crooked paths straight and rough places plain." No one was more prominently identified with the rival schemes brought forward between 1862 and 1864 for bridging the Tees, and thus connecting the two sides of the river. It will be remembered that Mr. Ralph Ward Jackson, the founder of West Hartlepool, proposed to carry the Durham and Cleveland Union Railway across the river immediately below Cargo Fleet, by means of a chain ferry, while the Stockton and Darlington Railway Company projected a Tees Bridge at Stockton, below the present railway bridge. A monster public meeting was held at Stockton, presided over by Mr.

Dodds, at which it was resolved to oppose both schemes. An inquiry afterwards took place into the two schemes, and Mr. Dodds was one of the most important and influential witnesses. The Tees Commissioners and the Stockton Town Council opposed both projects, on the ground that they would jeopardise the shipping interests of the port, and they had ultimately to be abandoned, to the great disappointment of their rival promoters.

The renewed attempt made by the North-Eastern Railway Company, in 1871, to obtain powers to construct a swing bridge across the River Tees, between Stockton and Middlesbrough, was again resisted by the Tees Conservancy Commissioners and the Town Council, and other public bodies of Stockton, South Stockton, and Yarm, and the evidence of Mr. Dodds before the Parliamentary Committee of the House of Commons, aided materially in securing the rejection of the scheme.

Mr. Dodds was one of the chief promoters if not the original projector, of the proposed new docks at Lackenby, the cost of which was estimated at over £300,000. This is a want which must some day be adequately supplied ; and, taken in combination with the enlargement and improvement of the old Docks at Middlesbrough—on which the North-Eastern Railway Company have expended a sum of over £100,000—and the improvement of the navigation of the channel, such extensive dock schemes would give to Stockton and Middlesbrough the most complete shipping facilities; and their ulterior, if not their immediate effect, would be to make the Ironopolis of the North one of the largest shipping ports in the Kingdom.

Mr. Dodds is also a director and one of the principal promoters of the proposed Cleveland Extension Mineral Railway, which has been designed to open out a virgin tract of ironstone between Skelton and Glaisdale, at present entirely excluded from the market. A bill with the same object was rejected by the House of Commons in 1872, but it passed through Parliament in the following session, and has become law, and the construction of the line will be proceeded with immediately.

In coming to speak of Mr. Dodds as an ironmaster, it is difficult to furnish anything like a complete inventory of the undertakings in which he is concerned; but of this there cannot be a doubt, that there are few in the Cleveland district who now hold a greater stake in the trade. His connection originated, we believe, with the formation of the firm of Stevenson, Jaques, and Company, about the year 1864. This company own the Acklam ironworks, which are situated about ten

minutes' walk from the Middlesbrough Royal
Exchange. They were started with three
furnaces, each 70 feet in height, 22 feet
diameter of boshes, and with a cubical capacity
of 17,000. In 1868, another furnace of the
same dimensions was added, so that the works
now consist of four furnaces, equal to the
production of nearly 1,500 tons of pig iron
per week. For several years subsequent to
this date, Mr. Dodds does not appear to have
sought to extend his connection with the trade
to any material extent; but the recent ple-
thora of prosperity with which ironmanufacturers were visited, and the consequent rapid
formation of companies established on the limited liability principle, led to his embarking still
more largely in industrial ventures. One of the
concerns in which Mr. Dodds is interested to
a large extent, and of which he is vice-chairman, is the Darlington ironworks, carried on
until 1872 by Mr. William Barningham,
situated at Albert Hill, and Springfield, near
Darlington. These works are, with only two
exceptions, the largest in the world, and are
capable of producing 100,000 tons of iron rails
annually. These exceptions are the Dowlais
works in Wales, and another establishment in
Staffordshire. The North Yorkshire ironworks, South Stockton, were commenced by
the firm of Messrs. Richardson, Johnson, and
Company, about 1864. They were carried on

by their proprietors until 1868, when they were acquired for the purpose of making steel on the Siemens-Martin system. After a very large sum of money had been expended in adapting them to this end, the system turned out a complete failure, and the works were stopped. Shortly afterwards they were taken up and re-constructed by a limited liability company, of which also Mr. Dodds is chairman; and they have since gone on most prosperously. The Tees Bridge Ironworks is another establishment in which Mr. Dodds has a very large stake. We believe, indeed, that he was the founder of the company by which these works were built; and he is now chairman of the directors. The Tees Bridge works are quite new. There are to be four blast furnaces in all, each 65 feet high. The site of the works is a piece of ground on the estate of Bowesfield, closely adjoining the bridge that crosses the Tees at Stockton. The Bowesfield ironworks at Stockton, is another concern in which Mr. Dodds is one of the largest shareholders, and the Stockton Forge Ironworks, Stockton, are, we believe, entirely his own property, and have been largely extended and improved since they passed into his hands.

In addition to the Boosbeck ironstone mines belonging to his firm, at which the ironstone has been won, and is now being

worked, Mr. Dodds and one or two other
gentlemen have secured and are about to
commence the development of a large and
valuable tract of ironstone at Girrick and
Moorsholme, on the route of the proposed
Cleveland extension line. Mr. Dodds—along
with Mr. Hugh Chaytor—has leased an extensive tract of land around Roseberry, for the
purpose of ironstone mining.

Recognising in common with many of the
leading ironmasters of the Cleveland district,
the necessity for further developing the
wealth of the Durham coal-fields, Mr. Dodds
in conjunction with four or five other gentlemen, of whom Captain Swan is, we believe,
chairman, has become the lessee of the Bear-
park coal royalty, situate upon the Lanchester
Valley Branch of the North-Eastern Railway,
within two miles of the City of Durham.
This most valuable tract of coal extends to
upwards of 2,000 acres, and promises to rank
with the best coal royalties of the district; and
to augment very largely the supply of coal.
Several coke ovens and workmen's houses have
been erected, and the number is intended to
be largely increased. We believe that Mr.
Dodds is also one of the partners in the
Mainsforth Coal Company, whose pits are
located near to Ferryhill, and of the Hutton
Henry Coal Company, who lately purchased a
portion of the estates of Mr. Milbank, M.P., and

also acquired the adjacent royalties of Marshall Fowler, Esq., the Rev. G. T. Fox, and others.

There are many institutions bearing more or less directly on the iron trade in which Mr. Dodds is interested. He is a member of the Stockton and Middlesbrough Chambers of Commerce, of the Middlesbrough Exchange Company, of the North of England Iron-masters' Association, and of the Freighters' Association, formed some months ago, to take combined action in reference to any question affecting the rates of mineral traffic in the Cleveland district. He was one of the earliest members and original promoters of the Iron and Steel Institute of Great Britain, along with several other north country ironmasters and members of Parliament.

The new turnpike road between Stockton and Middlesbrough, which reduced the distance between the two towns by three miles, owes its paternity to Mr. Dodds, who, in conjunction with his friend, the late Mr. John Shields Peacock, the esteemed and lamented Town Clerk of Middlesbrough, obtained the act, raised the needful funds, and finally opened the road during his mayoralty in 1858. Before the expiration of the Act, it is confidently anticipated that the remaining debt upon it will be discharged, and a free road presented to the district.

It is more than usually interesting to recall

the circumstances under which Mr. Dodds was first elected member for Stockton. His was the very first name mentioned for the seat when the general election of '68 was foreshadowed by the passing of the Reform Bill. A numerously-signed requisition was ultimately presented, requesting him to stand as a candidate; and he had the most encouraging promises of support from the most prominent members of the Liberal party in South Durham. His situation was a delicate and a difficult one. It was well understood that Lord Ernest Vane Tempest was to be a candidate in the Conservative interest, and Mr. Dodds had long been a friend and adviser of the Vane family. He was almost hand-in-glove with the late Marchioness of Londonderry, and with her son the present Marquis of Londonderry, visiting frequently at Wynyard Park, and occasionally consulted in arrangements of a business character in which his lordship was interested. His candidature threatened to involve a severance of this connection. But he was not deterred by the prospect of losing an influential friend and client. He boldly resolved to face all consequences and fight the battle of his fellow townsmen. The contest was a memorable one. Lasting for four months, or thereby, it was distinguished for its severity and its acrimony, but in the end the Liberal candidate

was returned by an overwhelming majority.
Despite the bolstering, the coaching, and the
blandishments of the Tory solicitors—for Mr.
Dodds is one of the few Liberal solicitors in
Stockton—the nominee of the noble house of
Wynyard was sent to the wall. The victory
was dearly purchased and deservedly won.
For months Mr. Dodds knew no rest. His
naturally excitable and sanguine temperament
was strung to the highest pitch of tension.
There were many vulnerable points to be
guarded, many a possible *coup d'etat* to be
checkmated. Those who were present will
not readily forget how he fought in the Re-
vision Courts, and before the Boundary Commissioners. The latter gentlemen were called
on to determine whether the Parliamentary
boundaries should be co-extensive with those
of the Municipal borough, or should include
South Stockton, which the Conservatives
wished to leave out in the cold. In a speech
of more than four hours' duration, Mr. Dodds
pleaded for the inclusion of South Stockton,
and his plea was ultimately successful. After
the election the hon. member was entertained
to a grand banquet, succeeded by a crowded
and enthusiastic public meeting in the theatre;
and the whole expenses of his election,
amounting to something like £1,500, were
subscribed for and defrayed by the constituency with a promptitude and heartiness that

has, probably, no parallel in the electioneering annals of this country, save that of the return of Mr. John Stuart Mill for Westminster.

At the general election in February, 1874, Mr. Dodds was again asked—at an influential meeting of Liberals—to represent the Borough, and for a time it was expected, on all sides, that he would be returned without opposition. Ultimately a section of the Conservatives—contrary to the advice of their local leaders—brought forward Mr. Francis Lyon Barrington, and after a brief contest, in which the Liberals did not deem it necessary to put forth their full strength, Mr. Dodds was triumphantly elected by a majority of 3,223, against his opponent who only obtained 1,425 votes. This decisive result was everywhere received with expressions of satisfaction, and it is believed that so long as Mr. Dodds cares to represent Stockton in Parliament, he will do so unchallenged.

Little remains to be added. The personal character of Mr. Dodds supplies the key to his success and popularity. Few men illustrate to greater perfection the *suaviter in modo* with the *fortiter in re*. There is no reserve, affected dignity, or *hauteur* about his composition. " How d'ye do, Dodds," is a salutation with which he is greeted on 'Change by those who know him least, as well as by those who know him best. His bland, benignant

H

manner invites freedom, and yet repels license. His blandness is thoroughly unstudied ; there is nothing of the *ars celare artem* about it; it is quite a part, and perhaps the most conspicuous part of himself. Probably, the greatest pleasure he enjoys is that of entering a ball-room or promenading on 'Change, or acting either as guest or host at a large party, in either of which, or in any other like circumstance, he dispenses nods, and becks, and wreathed smiles with a profusion, that would to many men be quite an ordeal. He is a fluent and effective, but not a brilliant speaker. His elocution does not take the popular ear by the use of rhetorical tricks. What he has to say, he says plainly, forcibly, and well; but the higher art of oratory—that which has won their fame for Gladstone and Bright —he has had no time to cultivate.

But after all, the most transparent feature of his character is energy. He never knew the luxury of *dolcè far niente.* Mr. Gladstone, at a great public banquet, once spoke of an idle man as the most miserable being on earth. One can easily fancy that under such circumstances Mr. Dodds would be such a man. For many years he has been accustomed to rise at six o'clock in the morning, and by seven he is hard at work, looking over and replying to his voluminous correspondence. His

travelling—and he travels many thousands
of miles every year—was always, and still
is frequently done during the night. To
facilitate his business arrangements, and
lose no time that could be otherwise employed, he succeeded some years ago in having
a through train put on between Stockton,
Middlesbrough, and London. This train has
since been known as "Dodds' Express."
During the session he habitually runs down
to Stockton, either on Friday night or Saturday morning, goes through the local business
of the week during Saturday, and returns to
town again on Sunday night or Monday
morning; or, if there is no important debate
or division coming on, he attends Middlesbrough iron market on Tuesday, and runs up
to London by the afternoon train of that day.

Allusion has already been made to the intimate relationship that existed between Mr.
Dodds and the chief ironmasters of Cleveland. He was the constant adviser of Messrs.
Bolckow and Vaughan, and he is a trustee
under the will of the latter. But his business
is not limited to his own immediate neighbourhood. Its far-reaching ramifications extend over the whole of the North Riding and
throughout the whole county of Durham, as
well as portions of Northumberland. Until
lately, the firm was carried on by Dodds and
Trotter, but the partnership having termi-

nated, Mr. Trotter withdrew from the business, which is now carried on by Mr. Dodds.

Shortly before last General Election a movement was set on foot, by a number of political and personal friends, to have the portrait of Mr. Dodds painted, and the requisite funds having been promptly subscribed, the work was entrusted to Mr. Jerry Barritt, the painter of the "Queen's Drawing Room," and other celebrated pictures.

In 1847, Mr. Dodds married Ann, daughter of Mr. William Smith, of Stockton, by whom he has a family of six—three sons and three daughters. The eldest son—Matthew Bowser Dodds—having taken the degree of B.A. at Trinity College, Cambridge, is now in the business, along with his father, and will ultimately take his place. The second son, Joseph Richardson Dodds, is studying for the church at Cambridge, and took the degree of B.A. in June, 1874. The third son, Frederick Lumley, having gained a scholarship in Durham Grammar School, which he held for five years, became an under graduate of Trinity College, Cambridge, and is passing through his studies with marked distinction.

VI.—EDGAR GILKES.

THERE is probably no one occupying so prominent a position in the North of England,
whose life, to do it anything like adequate
justice, would be more difficult to write than
that of Mr. Edgar Gilkes. The writer
approaches the task with a fear and diffidence
that he has not experienced in relation to any
of the sketches that have gone before. It is
not that there is any scarcity of materials to
work with, for few lives have been more
crowded with circumstance. But not many
of the events that will come under the notice
of the reader are of a kind that will live in
story or in song. They are rather the hard,
stern, and somewhat commonplace facts of a
laborious and useful life, passed in a quiet and
unobtrusive manner, and so circumscribed as
to area, that the reader who seeks for sensa-
tion or sentiment will turn to them in vain.

In the economy of human existence it is
often found, that while some men who have
done little to deserve honour or distinction,

bulk largely in the public eye, others of more
modesty and greater attainments are content
to "blush unseen." Those who have "borne
the burden and heat of the day" not unfrequently have their chief recompense in the
inward satisfaction "that passeth show"—
a sense of approval far more pleasurable than
the empty applause of the giddy and vulgar
throng. Much less of real, earnest, abiding
work is obtained from the man who lives in
the glare of popular admiration, and makes all
the aims of life subordinate thereto, than from
the silent, steady, plodding worker who "lives
laborious days," who is accustomed to burn
the midnight oil, and for whom the lines
appear to have been penned : —

"Men my brothers, men the workers, ever reaping something new,
That which they have done but earnest of the things that
they shall do."

These remarks are not offered by way of
justifying the position which we are compelled to assign Mr. Gilkes among the
pioneers of the Cleveland iron trade. In
speaking of him in this capacity, we are in
this difficulty, that we cannot lay our hands
upon any one great movement or event—discovery or revolution—with which his name
has been specially identified. And yet, it
would be even more difficult to evolve from
the ashes of the "dead past" a single pro-

ject matured in Cleveland that has not in one form or another borne the impress of his sign-manual. He has been a veritable Admiral Crichton, unwittingly perhaps, but none the less truly. Few men—perhaps no man—have actuated more powerfully the deeper and more essential springs of the society in which he has borne a part for the last thirty years. Traced to its source, we dare say that every public movement initiated in Middlesbrough during that time, will be found more or less to have owed its inspiration to Mr. Gilkes. If a meeting is held to utter a protest against some imperial iniquity, Mr. Gilkes will have been consulted by the promoters as to how it should be got up. If any social or local question requires to be ventilated through the same medium, the chances are ten to one that he has drawn up the resolutions. If an examination of a public school takes place, there again he will be found, hearing if not answering questions. The municipal affairs of the borough have been his special charge and mission since the population grew out of swaddling clothes. On commercial and industrial matters he is equally an authority and no less serviceable. In short, no man is more indispensable to that inner and hidden life which is after all the back-bone of prosperity in any community—the life that points a constant finger to the everlasting text that " man shall not live by bread alone "—the life that abnegates the gross, selfish, and materialistic elements that are too prone to germinate among a people eager to be rich, and privileged with exceptional opportunities for the attainment of that end.

Trained as an engineer in Berkshire, Mr. Gilkes, in 1839, came to Shildon, as one of the engineers of the Stockton and Darlington Railway. At that time the wide district known as South Durham and Cleveland was in a comparatively embryo state, both as to trade and population. The works at Shildon were also of very limited extent, for the whole rolling stock of the Darlington Railway Company did not exceed twelve locomotives—not one of which had a tender like the tenders of to-day, but a water-barrel and a coal wagon, one at each end of the engine—two or three hundred wagons, and about eighty carriages. These figures have since been multiplied more than a hundred-fold. In 1843, there was a branch establishment started at Middlesbrough, called the Tees Engine Works, for the repair of the rolling stock of the Stockton and Darlington Railway, and Mr. Gilkes came down from Shildon to undertake their management. A year or two later, Mr. Isaac Wilson and Mr. Gilkes entered into a partnership for carrying on the works under the firm of Gilkes, Wilson and Company, and from that time until the present the works have been among the most extensive and well-known in the North of England. Indeed, it may be said of these works, that they pioneered the engineering trade of the Tees. When they were originated there were only some half a dozen similar establishments between the Tees and the Tyne. These were the Gateshead Ironworks established in 1747; the Chester-le-Street Works, founded in 1793; the Walker Ironworks, established in 1809; the Forth Bank Engine Works, founded by Mr. Robert Hawthorn in 1817; the Hartlepool Ironworks, established in 1838; and the works of Messrs. R. Stephenson and Company, established at Newcastle in 1823.

For some years after they were founded, the Tees Engine Works assisted the works of Messrs. R. Stephenson and Company, and others, in making the locomotive engines used in the North of England. At the meeting of the British Association in Newcastle in 1863, it was reported that during the previous thirty-four years these firms had unitedly produced upwards of 2,400 locomotives. Probably no one contributed more than the subject of these remarks to develope the locomotive engine. He became early acquainted with both its merits and its imperfections; and at the works over which he presided all kinds of locomotives have been built, from the crude model furnished by Stephenson's Rocket, to the splendidly equiped and powerful engine of the present day.

But in the construction of viaducts and bridges, no less than in the building of locomotives, the firm of Gilkes, Wilson, and Company have taken a high position. At one time and another they have erected the Albert and Victoria Bridges in Windsor Park, bridges over the Thames above London, and the singular viaducts over the rivers Deepdale and Beelah, in Lancashire and Westmoreland. These bridges were constructed for the South Durham and Lancashire Union Railway. The Beelah Viaduct is constructed on a plan somewhat similar to that of the celebrated Crumlin Viaduct. It consists of 15 piers, composed of hollow columns. The span of the lattice girders forming the roadway is 60 feet. The total length of the viaduct is 1,000 feet, and the greatest depth from the rail to the ground is 195 feet. The quantity of materials used in its construction consists of 776 tons of cast iron, 303 tons of wrought iron, 12,343 cube feet of memel timber for roadway. Another engineering triumph of this firm is the celebrated viaduct at Saltburn, which is carried over the valley immediately in front of the Zetland Hotel, at the height of over 200 feet from the ground. In the construction of this bridge the firm were limited as to price, and

they exerted themselves to combine elegance
and strength with cheapness. They succeeded so well, that after the bridge was
finished it was declared by Sir William Armstrong, to be the cheapest construction—
having regard to its height and position—
in the world. But the firm of Gilkes,
Wilson, and Company have also produced
a large quantity of general engineering
work, including mill, colliery, and marine
engines, for nearly all parts of the kingdom.

In 1852, Mr. Gilkes commenced the erection of blast furnaces below the dock channel,
on what was then a piece of waste ground,
liable to the incursions of acquatic fowl.
These were the first blast furnaces built in
Cleveland after those of the Middlesbrough
ironworks, so that Mr. Gilkes is entitled to
take a position next to that occupied by the
late Mr. John Vaughan as a pioneer of the
Cleveland iron trade. The furnaces first
built by Mr. Gilkes had a cubical capacity of
only 5,500 feet, whereas the last furnaces built
at the same works represent 33,000 feet as
their cubical contents. At the Tees Ironworks
an interesting drawing may be seen exhibiting
the graduated growth in height and cubical
capacity of the different furnaces erected by
Mr. Gilkes—no less than five of the original
furnaces having been demolished and rebuilt
to a greater height within the space of twenty
years.

It is almost unnecessary to add that Mr. Gilkes projected the Tees Ironworks with the view of cultivating the advantage offered by the discovery of the Cleveland ironstone. But at that time there were only the mines of Messrs. Bolckow and Vaughan opened out at Eston. All beyond towards Thirsk on the one hand, and Whitby on the other, was an impenetrable *terra incognita.* Mr. Joseph Pease had acquired a royalty near to Guisborough, but it was practically valueless without adequate railway facilities. It was at this juncture that the project for the formation of a railway to Guisborough was formed. The local magnates pooh-poohed the idea. Even those who were likely to be the most directly benefited by having their estates opened up, turned a cold shoulder to the scheme. Mr. Pease foresaw, however, that the district was likely to become a great feeder to the iron trade, and that a large and valuable mineral traffic would thus be developed, so he came forward and offered to guarantee a dividend of 5 per cent. for a certain number of years if the line was proceeded with. Such an undertaking from such a source was the means of the ultimate construction of the line, and it is worthy of remark that it has fully justified the sanguine anticipations of its founder. The completion of the Guisborough Railway enabled Messrs.

Gilkes, Wilson, and Company to obtain ironstone from the mines that had been opened
up by the Messrs. Pease. Like other conscript fathers of the new industry, they had
at first many difficulties to surmount, arising
from the ignorance which then prevailed as
to the conditions under which the oolitic stone
of Cleveland should be smelted, shortcomings
peculiar to a new and unknown district, and
the competition they encountered from Wales,
Staffordshire, and Scotland. But " line upon
line, precept upon precept—here a little and
there a little," they overcame all the lions
that beset their path, and assisted to place
Cleveland on the high industrial eminence it
now occupies.

Before taking leave of the industrial phases
of Mr. Gilkes's career, it is only due to his
high attainments as an engineer to state that
he holds a most honourable place in his profession. Among his intimate personal friends,
he reckons many of the most prominent
engineers of the day, and although it has not
been given to him to take rank with Watt
and Stephenson, Bessemer and Arkwright,
as the founder of a new invention or industry
saving thousands and millions of pounds, or
employing armies of artizans, he has in his
quiet way contributed a large quota to the
perfection of engineering science.

For more than twenty years Mr. Gilkes has

been prominently identified with the municipal affairs of Middlesbrough. He sat in
the Commission that controlled the embryo
borough before it was incorporated ; and when
the charter of incorporation was granted, he
was one of the first elected to serve at the
new Council Board. With only a very limited
interregnum, he has continued ever since to
be a member of the Corporation, having passed the Mayor's chair and worn the alderman's
gown. As a member of the Council he has
devoted a great deal of his time to municipal
affairs, and he is still one of the most enterprising and active civic legislators of Middlesbrough. But the measure of Mr. Gilkes's
devotion to the public service is only faintly
represented by his work as a member of the
Corporation. As we have already indicated,
he is connected more or less intimately with
nearly every society, association, and institution in the town. He is likewise a borough
and county magistrate ; a member of the
Chamber of Commerce, a director of the Royal
Exchange, and a governor of the North Riding
Infirmary.

Although he has a considerable talent for
literature, Mr. Gilkes has not done anything
in this way to bring his name into prominent
notice. But we do not think it is disclos-
ing any profound secret, when we say
that he has from time to time produced verses

which would have done no discredit to a poet
of much greater pretensions, and although
fugitive and unrecognised, these verses have
in one form or another obtained a place in
several high-class periodicals. Of scientific
literature his pen has been rather barren,
although he has taken a somewhat con-
spicious place in the discussions of the
local Institution of Engineers, and the Iron
and Steel Institute, with both of which he is
connected, and has occasionally contributed to
the scientific and professional magazines,
papers which indicate at once the extent of
his information, and the power and precision
with which he could express it. We have
thus briefly recorded the simple facts ·of a
quiet life—which will be best understood in
after years, when the hidden facts, seen only
by the few and by the eye that sees all things,
are revealed in the light of that day which is
eternal.

VII.—JOSEPH PEASE.

Speaking at a meeting held to promote the candidature of his brother Henry, when the latter first stood as a candidate for the representation of South Durham, Joseph Pease said, " I have not a single drop of coward's blood in my veins." No one who knew the speaker could say otherwise. It is largely due to him and to the family of which he was for many years the recognised and honoured head, that South Durham and Cleveland have attained the position they now occupy. In the ordinary acceptation of the term, Joseph Pease was never an ironmaster; but it was he, and those who acted with him, that paved the way for the establishment and successful prosecution of the iron trade on the banks of the Tees. Full of sanguine and well-grounded hopes, he was at the same time animated by a spirit of determination and energy that persevered unto the end with whatever he took in hand. It was truly said of him that he could see a hundred years ahead. Not

only did he project "enterprises of great pith
and moment," but he invariably carried them
to a successful termination. From his earliest
years to the close of his busy career, he was
intimately associated with nearly every movement tending to the development of the
industrial resources of Cleveland. Next after
Messrs. Bolckow and Vaughan, the town of
Middlesbrough owes more to Joseph Pease
than to any other man. If to Bolckow and
Vaughan Middlesbrough owes its prosperity
and status, to Joseph Pease it certainly owes
its existence. For him, therefore, we can
claim an indisputable right to a place among
the pioneers of the Cleveland iron trade.

Born at Darlington, on the 22nd day of
June, 1799, Joseph Pease was the second son
of that Edward Pease whose name will live
in the industrial annals of his country as the
" founder of the first passenger railway in England." Mr. Pease received his early education
at Tatham's school in Leeds, and subsequently
Mr. Josiah Forster, of Southgate, near London, became his preceptor. Under this
gentleman Mr. Pease got something more
than a sound education. Mr. Forster was a
member of the Society of Friends—a persuasion to which his pupil also belonged—and
with much of the zeal that is characteristic
of that austere communion, he engaged in the
promotion of religious and political reforms.

I

His mantle fell not only on his pupil, but on more than one member of his own family, including his nephew, the Right Hon. W. E. Forster, with whom Mr. Pease in after life maintained a close and deep-rooted friendship.

The business career of Mr. Pease was inaugurated at an early age. While still in his " teens " he entered the office of his father, who at that time carried on, jointly with his brother, one of the largest woollen manufacturers in the North of England. Young Pease was trained to a practical knowledge of every department of the trade, and became an expert at sorting, combing, dressing, dyeing, the management of figures, or the routine of general office work. Edward Pease was a strict disciplinarian, and exacted from all in his employment, and especially from his son, the best work they were capable of turning out. Admonished continually that " whatever is worth doing is worth doing well," young Joseph acquired a methodical habit and an aptitude for business which, " if judgment were laid to the line and righteousness to the plummet," were certain in the long run to bring him to the top of the ladder. But while thus diligent in business, and bent on making a name for himself in the commercial world, he never acted the equivocal part of the dog in the manger. It could never be said of Joseph Pease that, having reached the top of the ladder, he drew it up after him, to prevent others from attaining the same goal; for, on the contrary, he was always ready both to spend and to be spent for the advancement and welfare of others. This, however, by the way. Before pausing to sum up his character, we are called upon to follow the fortunes of the Stockton and Darlington Railway, with the formation and whole history of which Mr. Joseph Pease has been prominently mixed up, and to the judicious management and opportune extensions of which the unique prosperity of the district through which it runs is mainly attributable.

The Stockton and Darlington Railway was only opened for traffic on the 27th day of September, 1825, but so far back as 1810 a committee was appointed to inquire into the practicability of forming a canal or railway for the better conveyance of goods and merchandise between Stockton and Darlington. Both Edward and Joseph Pease—the father and uncle of the subject of these remarks—were members of that committee, whose labours eventuated in the formation of a line commencing at Witton Park Colliery, and terminating at Stockton, its total length being about 27 miles. Between these two termini there were large and well-developed coal fields; but so far as the iron trade was concerned, it was as yet in the matrix of the future. Up to this point Joseph Pease had not interfered, except as a subordinate, in the schemes promoted by his father and uncle. But it was reserved for him to complete the work which they had begun. In 1829 a company of gentlemen became the proprietors of what has ever since been known as the Middlesbrough Estate. Young Joseph Pease—with whose fortunes from this time forward we have alone to deal—was the leading promoter of that company, which also included Messrs. T. Richardson, H. Birkbeck, S. Martin, Edward Pease, jun., and F. Gibson. The purchase only extended to 500 acres of ground, and at the time it was made there was not more than one or two farm-houses on the newly-acquired property. The land was used for agricultural purposes only, so that it was purchased at its then agricultural value, and although we cannot state the exact sum, it must have been comparatively trifling. But Joseph Pease and his partners had no idea of turning farmers. The far-seeing and constructive genius of Mr. Pease taught him to believe that Middlesbrough possessed rare facilities for the shipment of coal from the South Durham coal field, and he resolved to adapt the estate to this end. There were at that time only three ports on the North-East Coast from which coal was shipped on anything like a large scale. These were Newcastle, Sunderland,

and Blyth. The great South Durham coal
field was without an adequate outlet. The
first shipment of coal at Stockton took place
in 1822. In that year, 1,224 tons were exported. In 1828 this quantity had increased
to 66,051 tons. There were, however, in-
superable obstacles in the way of the development of the trade. The river Tees up to Stockton was only navigable at that time for the
smallest craft, which made the passage with the
utmost difficulty, and amid constant liability to
misadventure. It was Mr. Pease's idea that a
shipping port further down the river would
be much more suitable for the purpose, and
thus attract a much larger share of the trade.
He was not disappointed. Returns on which
every reliance can be placed show that the
opening up of the Stockton and Darlington
Railway exercised an important influence on
the trade of the former port, the shipment of
coals alone having increased from 1833 to
1840 at the rate of 157·57 per cent. as compared with those of 1828. But from 1840
Middlesbrough took the position which Joseph
Pease had predicted, and the trade of Stockton in the shipment of coals began to
decline as that of its rival advanced. We
find in the shipments of coal from Stockton
a decrease of 000·9 per cent. for the years
1841 to 1844 as compared with the three
years immediately preceding, while from 1845

to 1850 the decrease was still greater, being at the rate of 40·0 per cent. But while Middlesbrough has done much to injure the shipping prestige of Stockton, it is only fair to explain that it has been largely aided in this ungracious work by Hartlepool, which, although only commencing the shipment of coal in 1845, had increased the quantity of its shipments 76·6 per cent. between 1845 and 1850.

The Middlesbrough Estate having been acquired by Mr. Pease and his partners, the question naturally arose, how is it to be opened out? It came into their possession a real *terra incognita*, inaccessible on every hand except by the river, and even there the absence of docks or staithes prevented the possibility of utilising the place for shipping purposes. To many men, in like circumstances, the acquisition of such an isolated and forsaken territory would have been as bad as the present of a white elephant. But Joseph Pease had a settled and definite aim in view, and with the rationality and wisdom that distinguished most of his undertakings, he made all things subordinate to the realisation of that end. Until it could be penetrated by railway communication the Middlesbrough estate was worse than useless for his purpose. Hence he threw himself into the movement for the construction of the Middlesbrough

branch railway. After encountering a great
deal of opposition from the " vested interests "
of Yarm and Stockton, the Act was obtained
in May, 1828, for the extension to Middlesbrough of the Stockton and Darlington
Railway. In the conflict of opinion and
evidence that arose on this measure, Mr.
Pease rendered yeoman service to the cause
of progress. Although himself a coalowner—
not then on a large scale—his principal opponents were, curiously enough, neighbouring coalowners, who expected that the
opening of the proposed extension would
interfere with their monopoly, and otherwise
injure their trade. Mr. Pease lived to disabuse
their minds of this pernicious idea, and his
opponents were not long before they acknowledged their error.

The opening of the Middlesbrough branch
railway, which took place in December, 1830,
is a red letter day in the history of the
metropolis of Cleveland, marking an era
upon which all its subsequent progress has
more or less depended. The event was
marked by a ceremonial in which Joseph
Pease, as became his position, took a conspicuous part. From this time forward the
progress of the town was uninterrupted.
The coal trade of the port grew larger every
year, and employed a constantly-increasing
number of hands. From the time that rude

huts were first run up for the accommodation
of the navvies who constructed the line, and
the mechanics who built the shipping staithes,
the external accretion of the population went
on slowly at first, but none the less steadily,
until, when the first ironworks were established by Messrs. Bolckow and Vaughan in
1840, Middlesbrough had a population of
nearly 5,000 souls.

The Middlesbrough dock, which had not a
little to do with attracting the iron trade to
that part of Tees-side, was constructed by
Mr. Pease and Mr. Henry Birkbeck, of Norwich, along with one or two other capitalists.
It was afterwards sold to the Stockton and
Darlington Railway Company, on the award
of Sir W. Cubbitt, and Mr. Brian Donkin,
C.E. The formation of Middlesbrough as
the site of a system of docks and the terminus of a branch railway, was much opposed
by the late Lord Londonderry, and the late
Earl of Durham ; and it is probably not too
much to say, that the Middlesbrough Branch
Railway would never have been carried
through the House of Lords, had it not been
for the important service rendered by Mr.
R. H. Gurney, of Norwich, who being well-
known as a hunting man in Leicestershire
and his own country, induced a considerable
number of Norfolk noblemen and others to
come down and support the railway to the

new town. Several of the principal streets in
Middlesbrough, including Dacre-street and
Suffield-street, were subsequently named after
the noblemen who supported the Railway
Bill in the House of Lords. While speaking
of Mr. Pease's services to Middlesbrough, in
connection with the Railway and Dock, it is
only fair to add that it was owing to his great
exertions that the powers of the old Tees
Navigation Commissioners were taken from
them, and the control of the river vested in
the new Tees Conservancy Board.

Surely no apology is necessary for dwelling
so long on the pre-railway history of Middlesbrough and Mr. Pease's early connection
with that port. The circumstances above
recorded led up to the establishment of the
iron trade in the Cleveland district, although
their effect and tendency in that direction was
rather of a reflex than a direct character.
Joseph Pease and his partners forged one end
of the chain — the leading ironmasters of
Cleveland were responsible for the other.
Both were accessory to the development of
the district; but the one set only commenced
what the other has completed—if, indeed, it
is possible to speak of the Cleveland iron
trade as in any sense complete. Mr. Pease
and his co-workers made it their duty, as it
was their interest, to stimulate the growth of
the new infant Hercules by every means in

their power. They sought to recommend its advantages for industrial purposes; they increased those advantages in number and value. Above all, they were mainly instrumental in making it a centre of the iron trade. It was on the advice of the late Mr. John Harris, the then engineer of the Stockton and Darlington Railway, and Mr. Pease's right hand man, that Messrs. Bolckow and Vaughan were induced to establish their works at Middlesbrough. Mr. Pease offered every encouragement to the new firm, providing them with land on easy terms, and letters of introduction which proved of the utmost value in the way of giving their venture a fair start. Throughout the whole of their career, Messrs. Bolckow and Vaughan were on intimate terms with Mr. Pease, and there was between them a reciprocity of feeling and of interest that made the one rely to a large extent upon the other. We have heard it said, too, that there were pecuniary transactions carried on that reflected equal credit on both—proving, as it did, the limitless confidence of the one, and the honour and integrity of the other. It seems strange that Mr. Pease was never himself induced to go into the iron trade as a manufacturer. The most he ever did in this way was to acquire some ironstone royalties of which we shall have to speak presently. He was by inheritance a partner in the engine building

JOSEPH PEASE. 139

firm of R. Stephenson and Company, of
Newcastle. The works were originally founded
by the late George Stephenson, Robert
Stephenson, Edward Pease, and Thomas Richardson, the moiety held by the latter two
gentlemen descending to Joseph Pease, and
that held by the former two to the present
G. R. Stephenson, Esq.

Mr. Joseph Pease was one of the first to
understand the probable ultimate effects of
the opening up of the Cleveland ironstone, of
which Messrs. Bolckow and Vaughan were the
initial workers. They were followed in 1851,
by the Derwent Iron Company, who opened
out the Upleatham Mines on the Earl of
Zetland's property; and in 1853, Messrs.
Joseph Pease and his son, the present member for South Durham, commenced to open
out the Hutton Lowcross or Codhill mines,
near Guisborough. To develop this district,
an independent company obtained an Act of
Parliament for the construction of the Middlesbrough and Guisborough Railway, with
branches to Codhill and Roseberry Topping.
But such was the fear of railway enterprise
in 1851, so soon after the panic, that the line
was leased to Mr. Joseph Pease and Mr. J. W.
Pease, in order, under their guarantee of a
settled dividend, to raise the sum of £70,000.
With such vigour were the mines of the
Messrs. Pease pushed forward, that in 1856

140 PIONEERS OF THE CLEVELAND IRON TRADE.

they vended 217,253 tons of ironstone. Since
then, they have acquired the Upleatham and
Skinningrove Mines, and Messrs. J. W. Pease
and Partners are now the largest workers of
ironstone royalties in Cleveland.

It may be interesting, in this connection,
to give a few figures illustrative of the development of the district in which Mr. Joseph
Pease was the first to plant his foot, not as a
discoverer, but as a pioneer. In 1828, the
year that witnessed the commencement of the
Middlesbrough Branch, there were sent over
the Stockton and Darlington Railway 65,046
tons for export, and 64,739 tons of coal and
coke for landsale. In 1838 the total quantity
of coal and coke sent over the line was
654,787 ; in 1848, 1,044,202 ; and in 1851,
1,458,996 tons. It was in the latter year
that ironstone commenced to find a place in
the railway company's accounts. The total
quantity of ironstone sent over the section in
1851 was only 279,607 ; in 1862 this quantity
had increased to 975,810 ; and in 1872, it was
estimated at something like 4,000,000 tons.
In 1851, there were 120,604 tons of limestone
sent over the line ; in 1862, there were
427,091 tons ; and in 1872 there were close
on 1,000,000 tons. The traffic in coal and
coke has increased in a corresponding ratio ;
and in 1872, the total quantity of mineral
traffic sent over the section was, in round

numbers, close on eight and a half million
tons. It is almost unnecessary to add that the
great bulk of this enormous traffic is absorbed
by the iron trade of Tees-side.

The business so long carried on by the
firm of Messrs. Joseph Pease and Partners is
now one of the largest of its kind in the
North of England. In 1830 Mr. Pease first
became a colliery proprietor. In that year,
be became connected with St. Helen's Colliery, near Bishop Auckland, along with his
brother-in-law, Mr. Henry Birkbeck, of
Norwich ; the late Mr. Richard Hambury
Gurney, of Norwich; the late Mr. Simon
Murtin, of Gurney's Bank, Norwich; and the
late Mr. T. Richardson. About the same time
he acquired the Adelaide Colliery, near Shildon,
and subsequently he became a partner in the
South Durham Colliery, which, on the expiry
of the lease, was transferred to another company in 1846. His next speculation was the
Roddymoor Collieries, near Crook, which have
been greatly extended under his management,
until they now comprise nine different pits—
the Emma, the Lucy, the Job's Hill, the Bow-
den Close, the Stanley, the Wooley, the
Brandon, the Sunnyside, and the Esh. In
the Dearness Valley, Mr. Pease became the
lessee of a royalty on the property of Lord
Boyne, which led to the opening up of that
previously inaccessible region by the North-

Eastern Railway Company; and he also acquired another royalty at Hedley Hope, in the neighbourhood of Towlaw, which he carried on successfully for many years. For some time past, the firm of which Mr. Pease was the "head and front" has been producing about 600,000 to 700,000 tons of coke per annum. They are also largely concerned in the manufacture of fire-clay bricks, and other productions used in connection with the iron trade. So far as railway management is concerned, Mr. Pease was for the greater part of his life, and down almost to the day of his death, the most influential member of the Stockton and Darlington Railway. Opinions may differ as to certain conditions imposed by the directorate of that line with reference to its government—such for example as the prohibition of the sale of spirituous liquors in the refreshment rooms, and the excessively stringent precautions against smoking. But even those who are most prone to indulge a sneer at the "Quaker Railway Monopoly," and to affect contempt for the austerity of their conduct, cannot but admit that their management of the line, with which their names are indissolubly connected, has been eminently successful, pecuniarily and otherwise. For many years it has, with perhaps only two exceptions, stood at the top of the railway system of the United Kingdom as a valuable

property, in which respect it is improving
every year. But that is not all. The Stockton and Darlington Railway Board could until
1872, when an unfortunate accident happened
at Preston Junction, make a claim which
could not be made on behalf of any other
railway in England similarly circumstanced
—namely, that hardly a life had ever been lost
by an accident for which they could be held
responsible. In the whole annals of our
mercantile marine, there is only one line that
can make a like boast. We speak of the Cunard
line, which has sent ships from Liverpool
to New York and *vice versa*, at first twice, and
latterly three times-a-week, for a period of 40
years, and yet during the whole of that time
they have not lost a single life—not even a
solitary letter. In both cases, this wonderful
immunity from misadventure has been due
mainly to the skill, care, and foresight of the
management—which in the one case was presided over by Sir Samuel Cunard; and the
other by Mr. Joseph Pease.

It is not within the purpose of this sketch to
follow Mr. Pease throughout his political career,
which was both long and successful. He was
the first Quaker sent to the House of Commons. Returned to the Reform Parliament
in 1832, as the senior member for South
Durham, he was, in 1835 and 1837 respec-
tively, elected to the same honour without

opposition. He made his maiden speech on behalf of Mr. Joseph Hume's proposal for the abolition of lighthouses. From first to last he was an uncompromising opponent of jobbery, of corruption, of any and every unnecessary form of expenditure. Conformably with the peculiar tenets of the persuasion to which he belonged, he has always advocated the maintenance of a peace establishment, and set his face against war. Religious equality is another measure now almost completely realised for which he stoutly contended. Many a tough battle, both off and on the floor of St. Stephen's, was fought by the Quaker member on behalf of this, at that time, unpopular shibboleth. Whenever any question relating to the slave trade was brought on the carpet, Mr. Pease strenuously exerted himself to procure the abolition of that inhuman traffic. In 1841, finding his too scrupulous attendance on Parliamentary duties incompatible with the proper discharge of his numerous private obligations, he resolved to relinquish his seat for South Durham, and although pressed to reconsider his decision, he declared it to be unalterable. All testimony agrees in according to Mr. Pease the credit of being a regular attender of the House, a fluent and forcible speaker, an independent and noble-minded man. He was indefatigable in his attention to committee

work, and his large commercial knowledge
made him equally valuable whether as a witness or as a committee-man. On nearly every
committee appointed to deal with questions of
an industrial or scientific character he found
a place during his career in the House of
Commons. Of one important committee,
appointed to inquire into the subject of colliery ventilation, he was elected chairman.
That committee was appointed little more than
a year after Mr. Pease entered Parliament,
but after much research and enquiry they reported their inability to lay before the House
any particular plan by which accidents in
mines might be avoided with certainty, and
in consequence, they offered no decisive recommendations.

Mr. Pease sat upon a Committee on Church
Leases, which reported to the House of Commons on the 6th of May, 1836. He seems to
have taken a very active part in the cross-
examination of the witnesses, and to have
possessed very considerable knowledge of the
state of things in the county, especially
regarding the Dean and Chapter Estates.
With respect to the ecclesiastical properties,
that Committee reported its conclusions under
four heads, viz.:—No. 1. The abolition of
the injurious system of leases or fines. No.
2. The substitution of these for a fee simple
tenure. No. 3. The passing of an Enfran-

K

chisement Act. No. 4. The customary confidence of renewal by the lessees, to be considered according to local circumstances by
the authorities established under the Act, on
the principles of enfranchisement laid down
by them. These are the very points which,
nearly 40 years after, the Lessees of the Dean
and Chapter Estate of Durham are still de-
manding.

On Thursday morning, February 8, 1872,
Mr. Pease passed over to the great majority.
For several years previously, he had taken no
active part either in public life or the
private business of the firm. In his seventy-
third year, he met the shadow feared by man,
with confidence and resignation ; and Darlington, where he had lived for so many years,
was poorer by the loss of a wise counsellor
and beneficent friend. Joseph Pease was
not without his detractors. No man who as-
sumes the prominence which he earned can
hope to be. But whatever his failings might
be, " they leaned to virtue's side." His was
a large-hearted and whole-souled philanthropy
that was not to be influenced by any con-
siderations of " ancient use and wont." He
was an iconoclast ; but, after all, he built
up more than he destroyed, and he never
destroyed aught that promoted beneficent or
utilitarian ends. There was no temporising
in his nature. He never approved of half

measures. Vulgarly speaking, he went in for "the whole hog or none." He did this with such unflinching determination and success that his motives were often impugned, and his character otherwise assailed :—

> " All human virtue, to its latest breath,
> Finds envy never conquered but by death."

If success is to be accepted as in any sense the test of merit, then was Joseph Pease one of the most meritorious men of his time. He was a speculator, doubtless, but he speculated wisely and well. There was no gambling in his speculations. They were not dependent upon mere chance, or a fortuitous chain of events, although there was a certain risk attending them which he never shrunk from undertaking. Need we dwell upon the splendour of his conceptions, and their still more splendid execution? The enterprises he led, their results, and their *rationale*, the eminently practical character and tendency of his genius, the impetus which he gave to the railway system — these and many other achievements of his useful life will find a permanent place in the history of his native town and county. As for his bounty, if not like that of Juliet, " as boundless as the sea," it was measured only by his means and opportunities. He was not an indiscriminate giver, but yet there was no really good object that appealed to him in vain. Of the religious persuasion to which he belonged, he was long one of the most prominent leaders; while among the Liberal party in South Durham, his counsels were listened to with the utmost deference, and their action was often guided by his advice. Take him for all in all, it may be said of Joseph Pease :—

> " He was—but words are wanting to say what—
> Say what a Christian should be— he was that."

VIII.—W. R. I. HOPKINS.

ARDENT admirers of American institutions, sometimes put it forward as one of the greatest beauties of Transatlantic social life, that a man is not required to have a grandfather. In the old country a different state of matters is allowed to prevail. "Norman blood" is often a better passport to good society, than the "simple faith" which the Laureate has eulogised, and if it is known that the *débutante* in fashionable life is of plebeian origin, the damning fact operates as a bar sinister, which can only be atoned for by exceptional talents or conspicuous genius. After all is said and done, it is impossible to gainsay the fact, that the British public "dearly loves a lord." The growth of Democraey, notwithstanding, we have a warm corner deep down in our heart of hearts for old institutions, and hail with constitutional pride the scions of the great families who "came in with the Conqueror," or whose lineage can even be traced so far back as the period of the Renassance.

There can be no doubt that the unexampled growth of many of our modern centres of industry owes little to the fostering care of our "old nobility," whom Lord John Manners would preserve at the expense of "laws and learning, wealth and commerce." It is not unusual for the aristocratic mind to sneer at our captains of industry as *parvenu* and vulgar, while trade is contemned as demoralising and *infra dig.* Until very recently, therefore, the pioneers of our industrial progress were drawn almost exclusively from "the people," and patrician pride long held aloof from contamination with the industrial arts. But a change has at last "come o'er the spirit of their dreams;" and the highest and oldest families in England may now be found associated with the so-called plebeian element, in the development of our industrial wealth— as witness the relation of the Earls of Durham and Dudley with the iron and coal trades of Durham and Staffordshire. In this field of enterprise and competition the barriers of rank and caste are gradually being broken down; and the peer elbows the peasant in running the race for wealth—a race that is now more than ever open to all comers.

So far as the North of England iron trade is concerned, it owes not a little to those who could boast of having noble blood in their veins. The Marquis of Londonderry, the

Earl of Durham, and the Earl of Zetland,
have all more or less assisted its promotion.
But much more closely associated with its
development we find the name of Mr. William
Randolph Innes Hopkins, who is related to
one of the oldest and most aristocratic
families in Scotland, his father being a near
relative of the late Duke of Roxburghe, and
his mother being a member of one of the
oldest Border families. His father spent the
early part of his life " ayont the Tweed," and
it was near Kelso, one of the finest and most
historically and physically romantic of the
Border towns, where the son was born.
Transferring his residence to Darlington, the
father built and for many years lived in the
mansion of Woodside, afterwards occupied by
the late Mr. John Harris, the well-known
engineer of the Stockton and Darlington
Railway. Mr. Hopkins, senior, took an active
interest in the industrial progress of the
North, and was early appointed a director of
the North-Eastern Railway—then known as
the Great North of England Railway—an
office which he continued to fill for many
years, and to which his son, the subject of
this sketch, was subsequently elected. While
residing at his father's house in Darlington,
young Hopkins became apprenticed to Mr.
John Middleton, architect, with the intention of ultimately succeeding to a partner-

ship in his business. Lines and curves were, however, not to the taste of the young architect, and although he subsequently joined the staff of the distinguished Sir Digby Wyatt, in the preparation of the plans for the first Exhibition of 1851, he was not loth to abandon a profession in which eminence and emolument appeared so remote and difficult of attainment. The fact is, that the mind of young Hopkins had a bent towards the more comprehensive and widely-ramified art of engineering, rather than the more exact formulæ of architecture; and in pursuance of this tendency, he came to Middlesbrough in the year 1850, in order to superintend works established there for the manufacture of a commodity known as Warlick's patent fuel, which was then in much request. In this venture, the elder Mr. Hopkins was pecuniarily interested; and it was in connection with these works that the son first made the acquaintance of Mr. Gilkes, who afterwards became, and continues still, his partner in the Tees-side Ironworks, and other works " of that ilk." Circumstances arising out of the severe competition between patent fuel and the natural mineral compelled the ultimate abandonment of the venture which originally attracted Mr. Hopkins to Middlesbrough. He was the less reluctant to give up the fuel works, seeing that the Cleveland iron trade was then beginning to assume form, and to present the most tempting inducements to capitalists. Forming a partnership with Mr. Snowdon, an engineer who might be called a natural product of the north, inasmuch as he had formerly been an engine-driver on the Stockton and Darlington Railway, Mr. Hopkins made arrangements for going into the iron trade. Both partners had ample means at their disposal for that purpose. Both, too, had a rare combination of experience to carry them through, for Mr. Hopkins was an adept at figures, and was not unfamiliar with the principles of engineering, and metallurgical science, while his partner was a skilled engineer, indigenous to the soil, and knowing more than most men of the resources, facilities, and requirements of the district.

The Tees-side Ironworks were built by Messrs. Snowdon and Hopkins, in 1853. Eight years later the senior partner retired from the concern, which was carried on for some time afterwards under the style of Hopkins and Company, Mr. James Innes Hopkins and Mr. R. Lloyd, having meanwhile joined the firm. Another change afterwards took place, which resulted in the firm of Hopkins and Company being, in the year 1865, amalgamated with the firm of Gilkes, Wilson, and Company, of the Tees Engine Works, thus forming the gigantic concern of Hopkins, Gilkes, and Company, Limited, with a capital of £675,000, the management of whose affairs remained in the hands of the principals—Mr. Hopkins, Mr. Gilkes, and Mr. Wilson.

The Tees-side Ironworks have been the birthplace of many new and important inventions and improvements connected with the metallurgy of iron. As originally constructed, they comprised only rolling mills for the manufacture of bar and angle iron. Latterly they embraced also rail mills, and in 1857 two blast furnaces were built. The latter erections were 55 feet in height and 16 feet boshes, while each produced about 200 tons of pig iron weekly. In 1867, two additional blast furnaces, each 75 feet in height, were added. In the finished ironworks, there are 100 puddling furnaces, two forges, three rolling mills, and two blooming mills, placed in two different establishments in proximity to the blast furnaces. The weekly produce of the four blast furnaces is about 1,300 tons; while that of the mills being about 1,000 tons. About 2,000 hands are employed in the various establishments, and the amount paid in wages and salaries is over £3,000 per week. Among the mechanical improvements that have been originated at these works, engineers attach, perhaps, most importance to calcining kilns, designed by Mr. John Gjers, who was for several years engineer to the firm. These kilns are circular in shape and have wrought-iron shells, but unlike ordinary kilns of this class, the shells are made of the same shape as the interior of the kilns, so that there is merely a uniform thickness of fifteen inches of fire-brick lining at all parts. The shell and lining of each kiln rests upon an annular cast-iron entablature, which is in its turn supported by eight hollow cast-iron pillars cast on the base plate. By this arrangement a space is left all round the bottom for drawing the charge. The cubical contents of each kiln is about 5,500 feet, and the best testimony to the superiority of Mr. Gjers' invention, to the old square and cumbrous form of kiln formerly in use, is the fact that it has been very largely adopted in the Cleveland district. While employed at the Tees-side Ironworks, Mr. Gjers also devised a new form of hydraulic hoist, which has to a large extent superseded several other kinds of hoists used in the district; while the new system of water boshes, which the same gentleman was the first to use at the Tees-side Ironworks, not only enabled advantage to be taken of the cooling influence of the water, but renders it possible, from watching the temperature of the water, to tell exactly how the furnace is working, the segments forming separate water tanks.

It was at the Tees-side Ironworks where the first Danks's rotary puddling machine was erected in this country, and it is worthy of remark that in the subject of mechanical puddling Mr. Hopkins has always taken a lively interest. The experimental Danks's furnace was laid down at these works in the early part of 1872, and its first yield was watched by a large number of gentlemen connected with the iron trade in all parts of the kingdom. In reporting to the Iron and Steel Institute on the results obtained from this machine, Mr. Hopkins declared that his firm were not only satisfied with the economy of fuel and the absence of waste in every way, but they were also perfectly convinced of the superiority of the quality of iron produced. Indeed, Mr. Hopkins demonstrated so effectually the virtues of the mechanical puddler over the ordinary furnace, that it has since been largely adopted in the Cleveland district, and promises, unless something better meanwhile appears, to become the furnace of the future.

Besides his large interest in the Tees-side Ironworks, Mr. Hopkins is the principal partner in the Linthorpe Ironworks adjoining. He is largely interested in colliery and mining operations in South Durham and Cleveland; and he has inherited from his father, a talent for railway enterprise and administration.

Although his multifarious engagements have
prevented him from taking any very active
part in the deliberations of learned and technical societies, he is a prominent member of
the Iron and Steel Institute—serving on the
council of that association—and he is connected by membership with the Cleveland
Institution of Engineers, and the North of
England Mining and Mechanical Institute.
He was the first secretary of the North of
England Ironmanufacturers' Association, in
the establishment of which he took a leading
part. In this important office he was succeeded, some five years ago, by Mr. John
Jones, F.G.S., by whom it is still held.

Among other offices which he has filled for
a longer or shorter period, Mr. Hopkins is a
Commissioner of the Tees Conservancy, a
borough and county magistrate, a deputy-
lieutenant for the North Riding, a member of
the Middlesbrough Town Council, and a member of the Middlesbrough Chamber of Commerce. He was elected Mayor of Middlesbrough for two years in succession. First
appointed to the civic chair in 1867, it was a
question with the Corporation which of their
number could most fitly represent them
during the following year, when it was expected that the new Albert Park, presented
to the town by Mr. Bolckow, would be opened
by royalty. The choice of the Council

unanimously fell on Mr. Hopkins, who was accordingly re-elected for another year. Although the expectation that the Queen would open the park in person was doomed to disappointment, the town was honoured by a visit from Prince Arthur, whom his royal mother deputed to represent her on the occasion. The ceremony was attended by great " pomp and circumstance.'' Middlesbrough celebrated the event by holding high carnival. No fewer than six committees were appointed by the Corporation to carry out the arrangements, and on every one of them Mr. Hopkins served with zeal and unremitting attention. It was largely due to his tact and prudence that the event proved so eminently successful, and the very least that can be said about his conduct is, that he justified the choice of his colleagues in appointing him as their representative. Several other municipal events of importance occurred during the currency of Mr. Hopkins's mayoralty. Passing over those of minor interest, we are bound to refer to the general election of 1868, in which the newly enfranchised electors of Middlesbrough—which was created a Parliamentary borough under schedule B of the " Representation of the People Act, 1867,"—were called upon to choose their first representative. So far as the Liberal party were concerned, there was

very little difference of opinion as to who the
man of their choice should be. But while
it was felt that Mr. Bolckow had the first
claim to the consideration of the party to
whom he belonged, there was also among the
local Conservatives a widely diffused opinion
that Mr. Hopkins should be put forward in
their interest. At that time Mr. Hopkins was
in the height of his popularity; he was a
staunch and steadfast member of the Conservative party in the North Riding; he was
a fluent and effective speaker; and had the
Conservatives not felt themselves in the cold
shade of minority, it was quite probable that
he would have been put forward as their
representative. But in a constituency possessing such thoroughly Liberal instincts as
Middlesbrough, a struggle between a Liberal
and a Conservative could only have resulted
in the ignominious defeat of the latter. On
this account therefore, the party remained
inactive, although for a long time previous
to the election there were those who expected
that Mr. Hopkins would contest the borough.
As it was, he accorded a tacit support to Mr.
Bolckow, with whom he had long been associated in enteprises projected for the well-
being of the town and district, and to whom
he was attached by many social and commercial ties. In the General Election of
1874, Mr. Bolckow was opposed by Mr. John

Kane, of Darlington, and seeing that the seat was in danger of being wrested from Mr. Bolckow at any rate, Mr. Hopkins became a candidate in the Conservative interest. As might have been expected, he suffered defeat.

During the many years he sat in the Town Council of his adopted town, Mr. Hopkins was a zealous promoter of municipal reforms. He rendered yeoman service to the movement which resulted in the enfranchisement of Middlesbrough; he took an intelligent interest in the most trivial minutiæ of administration that fell to his lot, whether as a committee-man, or as a councillor and alderman; and he exerted to the utmost his not inconsiderable influence in order that Middlesbrough should not only maintain, but improve, the position she had attained as the metropolis of Cleveland. The Royal Exchange was projected while he was secretary of the Ironmasters' Association, and he had a principal hand in the carrying out of that important work. The North Riding Infirmary also claimed him as one of its founders. For religion and education he has done much—striving to uphold the influence of the Church of England, in a community where it was almost in danger of being utterly swamped, between heathenism and infidelity on the one hand, and the "dissidence of dissent" on the other. He and his fellow-labourers in this

sphere have been so far successful, that in spite
of the overmastering and prescriptive influence of Quakerism, and the less powerful,
although perhaps more aggressive tendencies
of Wesleyans and other dissenters, the Church
of England has at the present moment as
much real influence, and is doing as useful
and extensive work in Middlesbrough, as
any other denomination.

The highly cultivated taste for the higher
branches of architecture which Mr. Hopkins
acquired in his early years has never deserted
him. Some years ago he added another
charm to the many previously possessed
by the hill district of Cleveland, in the erection of an almost princely Gothic residence,
styled Grey Towers, with a beautiful out-look
towards Roseberry Topping, and the fine
highland range extending thence to the
Hambleton Hills. Built from designs furnished by Mr. John Ross, of Darlington, one
of the most eminent architects in the North,
Grey Towers and its demesnes have been extended year by year, gardens, plantations,
greenhouses, and extensive stabling having
been added, until now the estate and buildings
will compare favourably with any other in
the North of England.

Although few men have done more in a
quiet and unostentatious way for the advancement of Cleveland, there are few whose

L

lives, after passing through the same vicissitudes are so barren of materials for biography. To say that he has distinguished himself as a member of the Town Council is to say only that which may be claimed for many less able and less noteable men. To say that he has been on uniformly good terms with his workmen, showing an anxious desire for their welfare, and endeavouring to arrange all difficulties, not by the brutal arbitrament of strikes and locks-out, but by the "easy, artless, unencumbered plan" of arbitration and conciliation, is to award him a meed of praise due to other men who have been less remarkable in other ways. Nor is it much, perhaps, to say of him, *per se*, that he has been a liberal giver to good works, an enterprising capitalist, a zealous magistrate, a discerning and tasteful virtuoso, a keen sportsman, a devoted lover and patron of art, that he has taken an active part in local and imperial politics, that he is regarded as a pillar of the Church of England among those of his own communion ; that his gentlemanly and dignified bearing have provided for him a passport into society, in which many others, with probably more means, are unfit to mingle, that his sound and temperate judgment on all questions affecting the relations of capital and labour, and especially his extended experience at the North of England Arbitration

Board, give great weight to his opinions. It is not any one of these little traits, but the conjunction of the whole that make up the man, and stamp him as one of the most noteable and indispensable of Cleveland's aristocracy.

Mr. Hopkins has been twice married. His first wife was a sister of Mr. Bolckow, M.P. His second wife is a daughter of the late Mr. Hustler, of Acklam Hall, lord of the manor of Middlesbrough. He has a numerous family.

It ought to have been stated that Mr. Hopkins has ceased to be a member of the Tees Conservancy Board ; that he was honorary secretary of the Ironmasters' Association (Mr. William Gill being acting secretary); and, that although, serious mechanical difficulties have arisen with Danks's Puddling Furnace, the principle has been firmly established, and the difficulties will be overcome.

IX.—ISAAC LOWTHIAN BELL.

THE name of Mr. Isaac Lowthian Bell is familiar as a "household word" throughout the whole North of England. As a man of science he is known more or less wherever the manufacture of iron is carried on. It is to metallurgical chemistry that his attention has been chiefly directed ; but so far from confining his researches and attainments to this department alone, he has made incursions into other domains of practical and applied chemistry. No man has done more to stimulate the growth of the iron trade of the North of England. Baron Liebig has defined civilisation as economy of power, and viewed in this light civilisation is under deep obligations to Mr. Bell for the invaluable aid he has rendered in expounding the natural laws that are called into operation in the smelting process. The immense power now wielded by the ironmasters of the North of England is greatly due to their study and application of the most economical conditions under which the manufacture of iron can be carried on. But for their achievements in this direction, they could not have made headway so readily against rival manufacturers in Wales, Scotland, and South Staffordshire, who enjoyed a well-established reputation. But Mr. Bell and his colleagues felt that they must do something to compensate for the advantages possessed by the older iron-producing districts, and as we shall have occasion to show, were fully equal to the emergency.

Mr. Isaac Lowthian Bell is a son of the late Mr. Thomas Bell, of the well-known firm of ' Messrs. Losh, Wilson, and Bell, who owned the Walker Ironworks, near Newcastle. His mother was a daughter of Mr. Isaac Lowthian, of Newbiggen, near Carlisle. He had the benefit of a good education, concluded at the Edinburgh University, and at the University of Sorbonne, in Paris. From an early age he exhibited an aptitude for the study of science. Having completed his studies, and travelled a good deal on the Continent, in order to acquire the necessary experience, he was introduced to the works at Walker, in which his father was a partner. He continued there until the year 1850, when he retired in favour of his brother, Mr. Thomas Bell. In the course of the same year, he joined his father-in-law, Mr. Pattinson, and Mr. R. B.

Bowman, in the establishment of Chemical Works, at Washington. This venture was eminently successful. Subsequently it was joined by Mr. W. Swan, and on the death of Mr. Pattinson by Mr. R. S. Newall. The works at Washington, designed by Mr. Bell, are among the most extensive of their kind in the North of England, and have a wide reputation. During 1872 his connection with this undertaking terminated by his retirement from the firm. Besides the chemical establishment at Washington, Mr. Bell commenced, with his brothers, the manufacture of aluminium at the same place—this being, if we are rightly informed, the first attempt to establish works of that kind in England.

But what we have more particularly to deal with here is the establishment, in 1852, of the Clarence Ironworks, by Mr. I. L. Bell and his two brothers, Thomas and John. This was within two years of the discovery by Mr. Vaughan, of the main seam of the Cleveland ironstone. Port Clarence is situated on the north bank of the river Tees, and the site fixed upon for the new works was immediately opposite the Middlesbrough works of Messrs. Bolckow and Vaughan. There were then no works of the kind erected on that side of the river, and Port Clarence was literally a "waste howling wilderness." The ground on which the Clarence works are built was then flooded with water, which stretched away as far as Billingham on the one hand, and Seaton Carew on the other. Thirty years ago, the old channel of the Tees flowed over the exact spot on which the Clarence furnaces are now built. To one of less penetration than Mr. Bell, the site selected would have seemed anything but congenial for such an enterprise. But the new firm were alive to advantages that did not altogether appear on the surface. They concluded negotiations with the West Hartlepool Railway Company, to whom the estate belonged, for the purchase of about thirty acres of ground, upon which they commenced to erect four blast furnaces of the size and shape then common in Cleveland. From this beginning they have gradually enlarged the works until the site now extends to 200 acres of land (a great deal of which is submerged, although it may easily be reclaimed), and there are eight furnaces regularly in blast. With such an extensive site, the firm will be able to command an unlimited "tip" for their slag, and extend the capacity of the works at pleasure. At the present time, Messrs. Bell Brothers are building three new furnaces. The furnace lifts are worked by Sir William Armstrong's hydraulic accumulator, and the general plan of the works is carried out on the most modern and economical principles. As soon as they observed that higher furnaces, with a greater cubical capacity, were a source of economy, Messrs. Bell Brothers lost no time in reconstructing their old furnaces, which were only 50 feet in height; and they were among the first in Cleveland to adopt the Welsh plan of utilising the waste furnace gases, by which another great economy is effected. With a considerable frontage to the Tees, and a connection joining the Clarence branch of the North-Eastern Railway, Messrs. Bell Brothers possess ample facilities of transit. They raise all their own ironstone and coal, having mines at Saltburn, Normanby, and Skelton, and collieries in South Durham. A chemical laboratory is maintained in connection with their Clarence Works, and the results thereby obtained are regarded in the trade as of standard and unimpeachable exactitude.

Mr. I. L. Bell owns, conjointly with his two brothers, the iron-works at Washington. At these and the Clarence Works the firms produce about 3,000 tons of pig iron weekly. They raise from 500,000 to 600,000 tons of coal per annum, the greater portion of which is converted into coke. Their output of ironstone is so extensive that they not only supply about 10,000 tons a-week to their own furnaces, but they are under contract to supply large quantities to other works on Tees-side. Besides this, their Quarries near

Stanhope will produce about 100,000 tons of limestone, applicable as a flux at the ironworks. Last year, Mr. Bell informed the Coal Commission that his firm paid £100,000 a year in railway dues. Upwards of 5,000 workmen are in the employment of the firm at their different works and mines.

But there is another, and perhaps a more important sense than any yet indicated, in which Mr. Bell is entitled to claim a prominent place among the " Pioneers of the Cleveland Iron Trade." Mr. Joseph Bewick says, in his geological treatise on the Cleveland district, that " to Bell Brothers, more than to any other firm, is due the merit of having fully and effectually developed at this period (1843) the ironstone fields of Cleveland. It was no doubt owing to the examinations and surveys which a younger member of that firm (Mr. John Bell) caused to be made in different localities of the district, that the extent and position of the ironstone beds became better known to the public." Of late years the subject of this sketch has come to be regarded as one of the greatest living authorities on the statistical and scientific aspects of the Cleveland ironstone and the North of England iron trade as a whole. With the Northumberland and Durham coal fields he is scarcely less familiar, and in dealing with

these and cognate matters he has earned for
himself no small fame as a historiographer.
Leoni Levi himself could not discourse with
more facility on the possible extent and duration of our coal supplies. When the British
Association visited Newcastle in 1863, Mr.
Bell read a deeply interesting paper " On the
Manufacture of Iron in connection with the
Northumberland and Durham Coal Field," in
which he conveyed a great deal of valuable
information. According to Bewick, he said
the area of the main bed of Cleveland ironstone was 420 miles, and estimating the yield
of ironstone as 20,000 tons per acre, it resulted
that close on 5,000,000,000 tons are contained
in the main seam. Mr. Bell added that he
had calculated the quantity of coal in the
Northern coal field at 6,000,000,000 tons, so
that there was just about enough fuel in the one
district, reserving it for that purpose exclusively, to smelt the ironstone contained in
the main seam of the other. When the
Yorkshire Union of Mechanics' Institutes
visited Darlington in the spring of 1872, they
spent a day in Cleveland under the cicerone-
ship of Mr. Bell, who read a paper, which
he might have entitled "The Romance
of Trade," on the rise and progress of
Cleveland in relation to her iron manufactures; and before the Tyneside Naturalists'
Field Club, when they visited Saltburn in

1866, he read another paper dealing with the
geological features of the Cleveland district.
Although not strictly germane to our subject,
we may add here—that when, in 1870, the
Social Science Congress visited Newcastle,
Mr. Bell took an active and intelligent part
in the proceedings, and read a lengthy paper,
bristling with facts and figures, on the sanitary
condition of the town.

Owing to his varied scientific knowledge,
Mr. Bell has been selected to give evidence
on several important Parliamentary Committees, including that appointed to inquire
into the probable extent and duration of the
coal-fields of the United Kingdom. The
report of this Commission is now before us,
and Mr. Bell's evidence shows most con-
clusively the vast amount of practical knowledge that he has accumulated, not only as to
the phenomena of mineralogy and metallurgy
‘n Great Britain, but also in foreign countries.
Mr. Bell was again required to give evidence
before the Parliamentary Committee appointed
in 1873, to inquire into the causes of the
scarcity and dearness of coal.

In July, 1854, Mr. Bell was elected a
member of the North of England Institute of
Mining and Mechanical Engineers. He was
a member of the Council of the Institute from
1865 to 1866, when he was elected one of the
vice-presidents. He is a vice-president of

172 PIONEERS OF THE CLEVELAND IRON TRADE.

the Society of Mechanical Engineers, and last year was an associate member of the Council of Civil Engineers. He is also a fellow of the Chemical Society of London. To most of these societies he has contributed papers on matters connected with the manufacture of iron. When a Commission was appointed by Parliament to inquire into the constitution and management of Durham University, the institute presented a memorial to the Home Secretary, praying that a practical Mining College might be incorporated with the University, and Mr. Bell, Mr. G. Elliot, and Mr. Woodhouse, were appointed to give evidence in support of the memorial. He was one of the most important witnesses at the inquest held in connection with the disastrous explosion at Hetton Colliery in 1860, when twenty-one miners, nine horses, and fifty-six ponies were killed; and in 1867 he was a witness for the institute before the Parliamentary Committee appointed to inquire into the subject of technical education, his evidence, from his familiarity with the state of science on the Continent, being esteemed of importance. Some years ago, Mr. Bell brought under the notice of the Mining Institute an aluminium safety lamp. He pointed out that the specific heat of aluminum was very high, so that it might be long exposed to the action of fire before becoming red-hot, while it did not abstract the rays of light so readily as iron, which had a tendency to become black much sooner. Mr. Bell was during the course of last year elected an honorary member of a learned Society in the United States, his being only the second instance in which this distinction had been accorded. Upon that occasion, Mr. Abram Hewitt, the United States Commissioner to the Exhibition of 1862, remarked that Mr. Bell had by his researches made the iron makers of two continents his debtors.

Mr Bell is one of the founders of the Iron and Steel Institute of Great Britain, and has all along taken a prominent part in its deliberations. No other technical society, whether at home or abroad, has so rapidly taken a position of marked and confirmed practical usefulness. The proposal to form such an institute was first made at a meeting of the North of England Iron Trade, held in Newcastle, in September, 1868, and Mr. Bell was elected one of the first vice-presidents, and a member of the council. At the end of the year 1869 the Institute had 292 members; at the end of 1870 the number had increased to 348 ; and in August 1872, there were over 500 names on the roll of membership. These figures are surely a sufficient attestation of its utility. Mr. Bell's paper " On the development of heat, and its appro-

priation in blast furnaces of different dimensions," is considered the most valuable
contribution yet made through the medium
of the Iron and Steel Institute to the science
and practice of iron metallurgy. Since it
was submitted to the Middlesbrough meeting
of the Institute in 1869, this paper has been
widely discussed by scientific and practical
men at home and abroad, and the author has
from time to time added new matter, until it
has now swollen into a volume embracing between 400 and 500 pages, and bearing the
title of the " Chemical Phenomena of Iron
Smelting." As a proof of the high scientific
value placed upon this work, we may mention
that many portions have been translated into
German by Professor Tunner, who is, perhaps,
the most distinguished scientific metallurgist
on the Continent of Europe. The same distinction has been conferred upon Mr. Bell's
work by Professor Grüner, of the School of
Mines in Paris, who has communicated its
contents to the French iron trade, and by M.
Akerman, of Stockholm, who has performed
the same office for the benefit of the manufacturers of iron in Sweden. The first president
of the Iron and Steel Institute was the Duke
of Devonshire, the second Mr. H. Bessemer,
and for the two years commencing 1873, Mr.
Bell has enjoyed the highest honour the iron
trade of the British empire can confer.

As president of the Iron and Steel Institute, Mr. Bell presided over the deliberations of that body on their visit to Belgium in the autumn of 1873. The reception accorded to the Institute by their Belgian .rivals and friends was of the most hearty and enthusiastic description. The event, indeed, was regarded as one of international importance, and every opportunity, both public and private, was taken by our Belgian neighbours to honour England in the persons of those who formed her foremost scientific society. Mr. Bell delivered in the French language, a presidental address of singular ability, directed mainly to an exposition of the relative industrial conditions and prospects of the two greatest iron producing countries in Europe. As president of the Institute, Mr. Bell had to discharge the duty of presenting to the King of the Belgians, at a reception held by His Majesty at the Royal Palace in Brussels, all the members who had taken a part in the Belgium meeting, and the occasion will long be remembered as one of the most interesting and pleasant in the experience of those who were previleged to be present.

We will only deal with one more of Mr. Bell's relations to the iron trade. He was, we need scarcely say, one of the chief promoters of what is now known as the North of England Ironmasters' Association, and he has always been in the front of the deliberations and movements of that body. Before a meeting of this Association, held in 1867, he read a paper on the " Foreign Relations of the Iron Trade," in the course of which he showed that the attainments of foreign iron manufacturers in physical science were frequently much greater than our own, and deprecated the tendency of English artizans to obstruct the introduction of new inventions and processes. He has displayed an eager anxiety in the testing and elucidation of new discoveries, and no amount of labour or cost was grudged that seemed likely, in his view, to lead to mechanical improvements. He has investigated for himself every new appliance or process that claimed to possess advantages over those already in use, and he has thus rendered yeoman service to the interest of science, by discriminating between the chaff and the wheat.

For a period nearly approaching twenty-four years, Mr. Bell has been a member of the Newcastle Town Council, and one of the most prominent citizens of the town. Upon this phase of his career it is not our business to dwell at any length, but we cannot refrain from adding, that he has twice filled the chief magistrate's chair, that he served the statutory period as Sheriff of the town, that he is a director of the North-Eastern Railway, and that he was the first president of the New-

castle Chemical Society. In the general
election of 1868, Mr. Bell came forward as a
candidate for the Northern Division of the
county of Durham, in opposition to Mr. George
Elliot, but the personal influence of the latter
was too much for him, and he sustained a
defeat. In the general election of 1874, Mr.
Bell again stood for North Durham, in conjunction with Mr. C. M. Palmer, of Jarrow.
Mr. Elliott again contested the Division in the
Conservative interest. After a hard struggle,
Mr. Bell was returned at the head of the poll.
Shortly after the General Election, Mr. Elliott
received a baronetcy from Mr. Disraeli.
A short time only had elapsed, however, when
the Liberal members were unseated on
petition, because of general intimidation at
Hetton-le-Hole, Seaham, and other places—no
blame being, however, attributed to the two
members—and the result of a fresh election in
June following was the placing of Mr. Bell at
the bottom of the poll, although he was only
a short distance behind his Conservative
opponent—Sir George Elliott.

M

X.—WILLIAM BARNINGHAM.

THE founder of the great Darlington Ironworks—Mr. William Barningham—is in many
respects a remarkable man. He was born at
Arkengarthdale, near Richmond, Yorkshire,
on the 6th January, 1826, and is the youngest
of a family of eleven sons and two daughters.
Although the subject of these memoirs would
probably "smile at the claims of long descent"
quite as much as "the grand old gardener and
his wife;" and albeit, he may think with
Spurgeon, that ancient blood has little to recommend it, seeing that, go as far back as
you may, you come at last to the father of
the human race, "who was turned out of a
garden for stealing fruit," yet, it is interesting to record the fact, that the Barninghams
can trace their progenitors through a good
many generations. The family of this name
were the original proprietors of the village of
Barningham, on the Milbank property, south
of the Greta, and they have in this capacity,
found a place in Whittaker's History. Like
other old families, the Barninghams owned a

crest, obtained from the Herald's Office in
North Yorkshire, and bearing the motto
" Wonderful are the works of God." This
crest has been adopted by the Darlington
Iron Company, of which William Barningham
was the projector. In searching amid the
mists of hoar antiquity many curious reminiscences of the family may be found. Whittaker relates how one Robert Sutcliffe, who
held payment of some land from Easby Abbey,
offered to make restitution for some injury
done to Holy Mother Church, on the condition
that five holy abbots proceeded to the burial
place of his father and grandfather to pro-
nounce absolution. This condition was com-
plied with, and one of the abbots who assisted
in its fulfilment bore the name of Richard de
Barningham. But antiquity apart, we know
that the progenitors of Mr. William Barningham, were in humble circumstances, as their
" forbears " had been before them, and young
William was ushered into the world without
the proverbial silver spoon.

In the pretty little village of Arkengarthdale, William Barningham, like his brothers
and sisters before him, got the limited education that could be afforded him at a free
school—a school that was built and endowed
by one of the family of the well known Gilpin
Brown, of Sadberry Hall. When only nine
years of age, a circumstance occurred which

marked an era in the boy's life. His eldest
brother—the father of Mr. Thomas Barningham, managing director of the Darlington
Iron Works—had come down to the Dale to
spend a few days with his parents; and one
morning he sent his youngest brother to the
village of Reeth, to inquire for some letters
which he expected from Manchester. At that
time there was no daily delivery of letters in
the Dale. Unless they were sent for to the
village of Reeth, letters intended for the
·residents of the Dale where only delivered
once a week by coal carts, or by people who
went about the country purchasing farm produce. When, therefore, young William Barningham was employed to call at Reeth for his
brother's letters, he got instructions from a
number of the Dale folks to execute the same
commission for them; and these commissions
became so numerous, that in course of time
the boy came to be recognized as a sort of
post runner. The postage of a letter from
London cost at that time fourteen pence, and
this amount had to be handed over by the
party receiving the letter before it was given
up. For the letters which he undertook to
deliver, young Barningham was accustomed
to charge fifteen pence, the only remuneration
allowed him for his trouble, being a penny per
letter. That this was hard-earned money
may be judged from the fact that the lad had

often to walk as much as twenty to thirty
miles a day, and at the end of the week his
earnings did not exceed some 3s 6d or 4s.
But small as the amount was, it helped to eke
out the otherwise scanty earnings of the
family, and was probably a good deal more
than he could then have made in any
other way. In point of fact, the weekly
earnings of the boy came to be so much that
the postmaster refused to give him the letters
any longer, after he had been carrying them
for about a twelvemonth. This, to the young
messenger, was a crushing and unexpected
blow. Other boys of the same age would
probably have succumbed to the difficulty,
but to his mind it did not appear to be in-
superable. He sought the advice of a friend
named Anderson, the son of Gilpin Brown's
land agent; and after taking counsel together,
they determined to have a petition sent round
for signature among the Dale folks—to whom
the services rendered by young Barningham
were a real boon—and this petition was so
successful, that the postmaster agreed to re-
instate the plucky lad in his employment.
Facts like these, though apparently trifles
light as the thread of the gossamer, are yet
subtle and unmistakeable indications of the
spirit that was afterwards able to rise superior
to much greater difficulties. And, if there
are those who are disposed to inquire, as did

the mathematical student about "Paradise Lost,"—what does it prove?—we shall perhaps be pardoned for digressing so far as to add, that the circumstances which first tended in the case of William Barningham to prove that "the child is father to the man," were such as ought to inspire people of a later generation with most fervent gratitude, to those who were made the instruments of their removal—Rowland Hill and George Stephenson.

In 1839, young Barningham travelled with his mother to Shildon, in search of employment suited to his now more ample capacity and maturer years. They walked from Arkengarthdale to Shildon—a distance of twenty-five miles—on a Sunday afternoon. On the following day, they left Shildon for Middlesbrough by the old "Sunbeam" engine—one of the first locomotives built by Hawthorn, and one, too, which will still be remembered with interest by many whose youthful wonder and curiosity it helped to excite. Arrived at Middlesbrough, William found employment with his brother John in a small blacksmith's shop. It was at this shop that all the repairs necessary for the coal staithes at Middlesbrough Dock were executed, and on account of the engine employed to lift the coal wagons at the old staithes being broken, the youngster had to

work nine days during the first week of his
apprenticeship. In his case it could hardly
be said that " the wind was tempered to the
shorn lamb."

After he had been employed with his
brother for about two years, William Barningham began to display a genius for mechanics,
which sought every available means of development. On one occasion, he heard of a
number of castings of a mill engine, of the
grasshopper pattern, being procurable at
Stockton. Thither, accordingly, he went to
secure the coveted prize; and having received it, and returned to Middlesbrough, he
proceeded to adapt his castings to the construction of a small engine, with only a two
inch cylinder. Some of his friends having
been made acquainted with Barningham's
engineering efforts, a good deal of interest
was taken in the completion of the engine.
At last it was determined to give it a sort of
public trial. Steam was got up in a boiler
that was used by Mr. Cudworth (then a shipbuilder at Middlesbrough, but now engineer
of the Stockton and Darlington Railway) for
steaming the flanks of a ship's side; and the
trial was witnessed by Mr. Danby, then the
agent of the Stockton and Darlington Railway Company at Middlesbrough, and several
others. But, on account of the slides not
being correctly set, the engine only made

half a revolution where she should have made a whole one, and the trial was pronounced a failure. There happened, however, to be close at hand an engineman of the name of Gaiters, who saw what was wrong with the mechanism of the engine, and set the slides, so that it made about 500 revolutions per minute. Young Barningham was now as jubilant with success as he had previously been cast down with disappointment. His engine was shown to all his friends, and regarded as a prodigy of youthful capacity.

A very short time after this reminiscence, young Barningham resolved on spending a few days at his home in Arkengarthdale, and sent word to his mother that he was coming to assist her to churn by steam. The good old lady was rather bewildered, when her son arrived, to find him endeavouring to fulfil his promise. He got his engine conveyed to his father's house, and had everything necessary to set it in motion except a boiler ; but he was at his wits' end to discover how steam was to be raised. At last, he found about the old Methodist Chapel at Longthwaite, an elbow pipe which he thought might suit his purpose. He got this pipe plugged with wood, and having attached it to the engine, proceeded to get up steam by the aid of the kitchen fire. But when the steam had been got up, it had an effect very different to that

intended, for the plug was blown out of the
elbow pipe, and all the water escaped into the
fire, thus completely defeating the plans of
the young enthusiast, and compelling him to
abandon the novel idea of churning by steam
power.

Leaving his first engine at Arkengarthdale
to excite the curiosity and wonder of the
natives, young Barningham, on his return to
Middlesbrough, set about the construction of
a second engine with a four inch cylinder.
This second venture was considerably more
successful than the first. The engine became
the property of Mr. George Chapman, a
gentleman who is said to have built the first
house in Middlesbrough, and afterwards fell
into the hands of Mr. Isaac Sharp, formerly
agent to the Middlesbrough Owners. When
the youthful builder last heard of his creation,
it was employed in driving a turnip chopping
machine.

In September, 1843, and in the eighteenth
year of his age, William Barningham left
Middlesbrough for France, accompanied by
his brother James. At Middlesbrough, the
brothers Barningham had rather obtained a
celebrity in the manufacture of switches and
crossings for railway purposes; and they expected, no doubt, that they would be able to
find remunerative employment of the same
kind on the Continent. The Rouen and Paris

Railway was then in course of construction, by Messrs. Brassey, Mackenzie, and Company, and to Rouen the brothers repaired. They found, however, that Mr. Newman, the engineer of the line, had gone on to Paris,—a distance of over a hundred miles—and they were obliged to follow him there. Taking the boat down the Seine, the brothers found at Paris that they had undertaken a fruitless journey, Mr Newman having just left for Rouen. They waited his arrival in Paris for a week, and were then discouraged by hearing from him that the whole of the work connected with the line had been let to M. M. Alcard, Buddicombe and Company, of the Chatreux Iron Company, near Rouen. Determined, however, that they would not abandon their object, they proceeded back to Rouen, and called at the Chatreux Works. Their satisfaction may be imagined when they found that the manager of these works was a Mr. Whalley, who had formerly been manager at the works of Neasham and Welch, Stockton-on-Tees. But Mr. Whalley informed them that he saw little probability of being able to do anything for them. The work for which they applied had been let to others a few days previously; and there was no other railway then under construction in France that afforded any likelihood of employment. James Barningham proposed that they should return to England; but William could not brook the idea of failure, and declared that rather than go back again, he would work his way on board a steamer from Havre to America. They were not obliged to adopt either alternative. Messrs. Brassey and Mackenzie offered them work in connection with the permanent way department of the new Rouen and Paris line. Their business was that of straightening the rails that had been bent and injured in course of transit from South Wales. At this work they were employed for some six months, when the owners of the Chatreux Works offered them the employment for which they had originally made application, and for six months more they made the switches and crossings for the new line. At the end of that time James Barningham returned to England, but he could not persuade William to accompany him. The latter had conceived the idea of making switches and crossings out of rails and railway chairs in separate sections, instead of having them all in one piece. This idea he laid before Mr. John Jones, manager to Messrs. Brassey, Mackenzie, and Company. Mr. Jones was so much struck with the feasibility and advantages of the plan proposed, that he built for its author a workshop at a place called Maloney, near Rouen, and put him in charge of several men who had this work in hand.

The results obtained were so satisfactory that Mr. Barningham was able to realise a net profit of £40 per month. At this time, he was only nineteen years of age, although his appearance conveyed the impression that he was considerably older ; and considering the exceptional position he occupied, he was extremely careful to conceal his juvenility from those with whom he came into contact. After enjoying this run of prosperity for six months, Mr. Barningham found his income gradually falling off, in consequence of the payment of reduced prices, until it only reached £20 per month; and thinking, probably, that there was little chance of further improving his position by remaining in France, he determined to return to England.

Three brothers of Mr. Barningham were at this time employed in Manchester, and to them William suggested the project of opening in that city a foundry, specially adapted for colliery work. This foundry was established and carried on for about eighteen months, but without success, William having lost in the venture a great part of the money he had saved in France. In the course of a visit which he made to the Cleveland district, after the abandonment of the Manchester foundry, Mr. Barningham met Mr. John Harris, engineer and contractor for the maintenance of the permanent way of the Stockton

and Darlington Railway, and engineer for the
Wakefield and Goole Railway. In consequence of an interview between Mr. Harris
and Mr. Barningham, it was determined that
the latter should come to Middlesbrough and
establish works for the manufacture of railway switches and crossings. These works
were built on the site now occupied by the
rolling mills of Hopkins, Gilkes, and Company.
Mr. Barningham was at this time about
totally destitute of means, but he had met at
a temperance hotel, where he resided in Middlesbrough, a Blyth shipowner named James
Brown, who took a considerable interest
in his plans, and advanced him a sum
of £1,000, to enable him to carry on
works at Middlesbrough, without requiring security for the loan. Fortunately
the Middlesbrough Works turned out a successful undertaking, and in consideration of
his kindness, Mr. Brown was admitted into
partnership.

While travelling about the country in
search of orders for his works at Middlesbrough, Mr. Barningham was struck with the
fact that large quantities of worn out iron
rails were lying about the works of the Lancashire and Yorkshire Railway Company, at
Manchester. These rails were then sent
back to be re-manufactured at the different
works in Staffordshire, Wales, and Scotland,

where they were made. It appeared perfectly evident, that to carry these old rails to either of these districts, and bring them back again to Manchester, would represent a heavy cost for carriage. With the object of ascertaining whether this cost could not be avoided, by the establishment at Manchester of works for the re-manufacture of used-up rails, Mr. Barningham waited on Admiral Lows, the general manager of the Lancashire and Yorkshire Railway, who was convinced of the practicability and value of the idea, and offered every inducement to Mr. Barningham in order that he might be induced to undertake the erection of such works. He even went the length of recommending an excellent site for the proposed works, between the canal and the railway at Pendleton, just outside Manchester ; and committed the Lancashire and Yorkshire Railway Company to a contract for the re-manufacture of 4,000 tons of rails, and 2,000 tons of railway chairs, when the works should be established. This was the origin of the great Pendleton Iron Works, which have been carried on by Mr. Barningham since that time with unvarying success.

After the Pendleton Works had been some time in operation, the attention of Mr. Barningham was attracted to the advantages presented by the new iron making district of

Cleveland, for the economical production of iron rails. His friend Mr. Brown was the first to call Mr. Barningham's attention to this matter, by quoting from newspapers and other sources paragraphs dealing with the requirements of the different railway companies throughout the world. One contract for 50,000 tons of rails was advertised by the East India Railway Company; and the owner of the Pendleton Works, although he should have liked to put in a quotation for this contract, was not in a position to do so. Apart from its limited size, the geographical position of the Pendleton Works unfitted them for carrying on the manufacture of rails on a large scale. Ultimately, therefore, Mr. Barningham resolved on the establishment of works in Cleveland. In pursuance of this resolution, he visited the district, and several sites suitable for his purpose were pointed out to him by Mr. Samuel Chester, late manager of the West Hartlepool Railway. But Mr. Barningham saw no locality so well adapted to his purpose as Albert Hill, Darlington. On the main line between London and the North, and having excellent facilities for reaching shipping ports on the North-East coast, it was also placed in close proximity to the South Durham blast furnaces, from which the pig iron could be obtained free of any freightage charges. Some time afterwards, he met the late Mr. Frank Harker, then manager of the South Durham blast furnaces, and the late Mr. John Harris, the then engineer of the Stockton and Darlington Railway. To these gentlemen Mr. Barningham unfolded his views, taking care, however, to keep them ignorant of his selection of Albert Hill as the site of his proposed works. When he had returned to Darlington, Mr. Harker saw Mr. Henry Pease, one of the then directors of the South Durham Ironworks, and informed him of Mr. Barningham's intentions. Discerning that such works could be worked in profitable conjunction with the South Durham blast furnaces, Mr. Pease endeavoured to persuade Mr. Barningham to erect his works on Albert Hill ; and the latter, on receiving an offer of 4½ acres of land at £350 per acre, with an option as to the purchase of other eight acres at £300 per acre, agreed to comply with the invitation. It is seventeen years last April since Mr. Barningham visited the North to select a site for his proposed new works, and by April of the following year, the works were far advanced towards completion. The site, however, appeared to be so circumscribed, and the projector had such large ideas of further development that he shortly afterwards purchased the Springfield farm, eight-five acres in extent, for a sum of £11,000 ; and as illustrat-

ing the enormous increase in the value of
property within the last fifteen years, we may
add here that ground in the same locality
has recently been bought for £1,000 per
acre.

The first contract undertaken by Mr. Barningham, after the Albert Hill Works were
completed, was an order for the permanent
way of a railway between Calcutta and Port
Canning, twenty-one miles in length. This
was followed shortly afterwards by a contract
for the great bulk of the rails necessary to
lay the Eastern Bengal Railway, 160 miles in
length. For every railway in India, except
the Bombay and Baroada, and the great
Indian and Peninsular, the rails have been
supplied either in whole or in part by Mr.
Barningham; while no name is better known
among the railway interests of America. A
great portion of the rails required for the
Pacific line, were made at the Albert Hill
Works; and while he had this work on hand,
Mr. Barningham became necessarily involved
in large financial transactions with the notori-
ous Jay Cooke and his friends. In 1867 Mr.
Baruingham concluded a contract with the
Imperial Government of Russia for the supply
of 6,000 tons of rails; and some little time
afterwards he was asked to supply the rails
for the Czar's private railway to Sarscasils.
In connection with these important contracts,

N

Mr. Barningham paid a visit to Russia in 1868, and at St. Petersburg he had an interview with General Melinkoff, the Minister of Public Works, who strongly advised him to establish ironworks, near to Taganrog, on the sea of Azoff, in Southern Russia. The inducements held out to the adoption of this course were so tempting, that Mr. Barningham had actually proceeded as far as Moscow with the view of making a survey of the district round about Taganrog, and ascertaining its rescources for the carrying on of works, as suggested by General Melinkoff; but pressing business necessitated his return to England, before he could carry out his plans in reference to Russia. The project has since been carried out by an Englishman named Hughes, aided by the late Mr. Thomas Brassey, and a handsome subsidy from the Imperial Treasury ; and the works are said to be very successful.

Enough has been said in the earlier part of this biography to show that Mr. Barningham has always had a talent for mechanics. He is the patentee of a valuable invention which was highly approved of by the late Mr. Brunel; an engineer of European fame, and has been adopted on the Australian and other railways. It consists in the combination of two railway fishes and two railway chairs, in separate pieces, thus forming a girder from sleeper to sleeper. Another novel idea of Mr. Barningham's, although it has not yet been practically adopted, was illustrated for some years on the walls of the Stockton and Darlington Railway Station at the latter town. Mr. Barningham proposed to feed blast furnaces by running the trucks filled with the raw material up an incline, and then allowing them to pass over the furnace, dropping their contents into the furnace as they did so, instead of distributing the material in barrowfuls as at present, thus avoiding the cost of hoisting it to the top of the furnace in small quantities. If the idea were practicable—and we do not say that it is not—it would undoubtedly lead to a great economy in blast furnace operations; but no blast furnace engineer has yet been induced to make the attempt.

XI.—DAVID DALE.

THE name of Mr. David Dale will always be associated more, perhaps, than any other with the Board of Arbitration and Conciliation, established in 1869, for the settlement of disputes arising in connection with the North of England iron trade. Of that highly useful tribunal he was one of the original and most active promoters, and since its formation he has been its first and only President. But there are many other phases in Mr. Dale's career closely interwoven with the development of the iron trade of Cleveland. Railway management has received a large share of his attention. Mining enterprise has likewise been indebted to his labours. His financial talents have repeatedly been called into requisition in almost hopeless cases of emergency ; and at the present time he occupies a position of prominent usefulness and influence subordinate to none in the district with which he is connected.

Mr. Dale was born in British India. His father was judge of the City Court of Moorshadabad, in the East India Company's Bengal service. His grandfather was the brother of that David Dale who founded the New Lanark Mills, near Glasgow, and of whom his· grandson, Robert Dale Owen, has recently recorded many interesting reminiscences in the *Atlantic Monthly*. While he was yet an infant the subject of this biography left India in the company of his father and mother, but the former died on the voyage home. Arrived in England, Mrs. Dale took the route to New Lanark, intending to sojourn for a time with her husband's friends there. An accident to the mail coach when within a few miles of Darlington, caused her such serious injuries that she was unable to proceed further. Friendless and alone, she had no private house to fall back upon, and was therefore necessitated to put up at the King's Head, in Darlington, where she met with so much kindness and attention from some of the " Friends," as induced her shortly afterwards to return and settle in that town. Thus it was, in a purely accidental way, that Mr. Dale became connected with Darlington.

Commencing his business career in the office of the Stockton and Darlington Railway Company, under the late Mr. Macnay, Mr. Dale had been accustomed from his earliest years to understand and deal with the special requirements of the Cleveland district. He

showed such conspicuous business aptitude
that when little more than twenty years of
age, he was appointed secretary to the Mid-
·dlesbrough and Guisborough section of the
Stockton and Darlington system. After occupying for six ·years a secretarial position,
he entered into partnership with Mr. W.
Bouch, and became part lessee of the Shildon
Locomotive Works, at the village of that
name, distant about six miles from Darlington. Under an arrangement with the Board
of the Darlington and Stockton section, the
working of that line was done by contract
with Messrs. Bouch and Dale, carrying on
business as the Shildon Works Company.
This was an undertaking of a very responsible and extensive kind, the heavy mineral
traffic of the Darlington section requiring
much skill and care in its management. But
it was also a prosperous enterprise, as, indeed,
it could hardly fail to be under the control of
two gentlemen so eminently qualified to carry
it on. Mr. Bouch is an engineer of large
experience and exceptional attainments.· Lo·
comotive engineering owes to his ingenuity
many improvements of the most valuable
kind. He has patented a new application of
reversing gear, which enables an engine to be
drawn up while running full speed without
knocking off steam ; and this device, when
exhibited by Mr. Stephenson at the last Paris

Exhibition, attracted much attention from the engineering profession. Another invention of Mr. Bouch's is a patent steam retarder, which acts as an efficient brake, by admitting steam on each side of the piston. Both of these improvements and several others that owe their paternity to the same gentleman are now applied to all the engines built for the Stockton and Darlington system. It was Mr. Bouch's business under the co-partnery agreement to look after the practical working while Mr. Dale attended to financial arrangements and correspondence. The Shildon Works grew and prospered to such an extent, that their *localè* had to be removed a few years ago from Shildon to Darlington. The new works have been built on a very extensive scale. They give employment to over 1,000 hands, not only in the maintenance of the large stock of locomotives belonging to the Darlington section, but in the building of many new engines to keep that stock up to the highest point of efficiency. Three of the last passenger engines built have each two cylinders 17 inches diameter and a stroke of 30 inches. They work at a boiler pressure of 140 lbs. per square inch. The driving wheels are 7 feet diameter, and the maximum speed attainable is 70 miles an hour. Owing to their enormous size and power, these engines have been styled " Ginx's Babies." The arrange-

ment under which Mr. Dale became connected
with the Shildon works terminated three or
four years ago, and now the locomotive management is conducted under rather different
conditions, although the Darlington section
still depends upon these works for all their
locomotive power.

Mr. Dale's connection with the iron trade of
the North of England commenced in 1857. On
the stoppage of the Northumberland and Durham District Bank in that year, the Derwent
Iron Company, to whom the Consett Iron Works
belonged, became insolvent. Mr. Dale was
then appointed, in conjunction with Mr. J. W.
Pease, M.P., and the late Colonel Stobart, of
Etherley, one of the inspectors under whose
control the Consett works were to be carried
on by Mr. Jonathan Richardson on behalf of
the creditors. The affairs of the company
were in a very involved condition; and as
Mr. Dale was the really responsible inspector,
(his colleagues being simply consulted on
matters of the utmost moment), his appointment was anything but a sinecure. The
office, however, was not one of long duration.
The arrangement made with Mr. Richardson
was superseded on the purchase of the works
at Consett by the Derwent and Consett Iron
Company, of whom Mr. Allhusen, of Newcastle, Mr. Jonathan Priestman, and Mr.
Joseph Hawks were the managing directors.

Owing, however, to the Derwent and Consett Iron Company being unable to complete their purchase, the works again came into the market after about two years possession by that proprietary, and the present company was then formed in April, 1864, with a capital of £400,000, divided into 40,000 shares of £10 each, Mr. Dale and Mr. Priestman being appointed managing directors. Of this amount, only £295,318 was paid for the works, plant, and royalties owned by the old company. Considering the immense extent of the concern, the purchase was a decidedly cheap one, although none of the eighteen furnaces then built were adapted to the modern requirements of the trade ; and they have all been since demolished. In September, 1866, the company purchased the adjoining works of the Shotley Bridge Iron Company, and thereupon created 6,000 additional shares of £10 each, making £60,000 additional capital. In September, 1872, 9,200 additional shares, of the nominal value of £10 each, were allotted to the then proprietors out of the revenue of the company, £7 10s per share being paid at once on each new creation of capital.

It would be impossible to find in the whole industrial experience of this country, a greater contrast than that presented by the Consett Iron Works under their past and present management. The undertaking was originally one of the most gigantic of its kind in the United Kingdom, for there are no ironworks even at the present day that can boast of so many as eighteen blast furnaces. The rock upon which the Derwent Company split would appear to be that of developing their concern too rapidly. They experienced the fate that proverbially attends " vaulting ambition "— they " o'erleaped themselves and fell on t'other side." Their case was by no means singular. The Ayrshire Ironworks, in Scotland, " fell from its high estate," from kindred causes, and the plant, etc., which originally cost close on £100,000, had to be disposed of in liquidation for the miserably inadequate sum of £20,000. Both of these concerns came to grief in the same panic ; but both had undoubtedly internal and probably insurmountable elements of weakness, apart from the final crash that laid them prostrate. Under the new *regimé* the Consett works have enjoyed a large and uninterrupted run of prosperity. From the formation of the company, in 1864, until the 30th June, 1870, the dividends of the company averaged 10 per cent. after defraying the cost of building six large blast furnaces out of revenue, and making other considerable improvements and additions to the works. Since 1870, the dividends paid to the shareholders have been even higher. At the present time it is unquestionably one of the most substantial and flourishing concerns in the North of England. The company own large coal royalties, from which they raise sufficient to supply the whole of their own blast furnaces, mills, and forges, and leave a considerable surplus for sale. They are also exceptionally well off as regards the supply of other minerals. Their predecessors—the Derwent Iron Company—formerly owned the celebrated Stanhope Limestone Quarries, which were sold to the Stockton and Darlington Railway Company, subject to the supply of the Consett works, for many years, at a very low figure. In like manner, the Derwent Company owned the Upleatham ironstone mines in Cleveland; and these were disposed of to Messrs. J. and J. W. Pease and Partners, on the formation of the new proprietary, under similar conditions. More than any other firm in the Cleveland district, the Consett Iron Company make use of the hematite ores of Cumberland and Westmorland, this quality being the most suitable for the manufacture of ship plates, which is the staple produce of these works. The increasing scarcity of the Cumberland hematite, has led the Company within the last two years, to enter into arrangements for the acquisition and development of large hematite royalties at

Bilbao, in Spain, in conjunction with the Dowlais Iron Company and the celebrated Prussian gunmaker, Mr. Krupp, of Essen.

The Consett Company give employment to between 5,000 and 6,000 work people. They have now six blast furnaces in operation, each capable of producing 450 tons of pig iron per week. It was at these works that Whitwell's patent fire-brick hot blast stoves were first fitted up, and it will be remembered that the patentee, at the Dudley meeting of the Iron and Steel Institute, read a paper containing much interesting information as to the results obtained from the use of his stoves at Consett. The crude pig iron manufactured at Consett is almost entirely used in the mills and forges adjacent. In the puddling department there are 150 furnaces, two forge engines, five steam hammers, and all other necessary appliances for the turn out of a large quantity of work. In their speciality of ship plates the Consett Iron Company make more than any other individual firm in the country. Four out of the five rolling mills in operation are exclusively engaged on ship plates, the fifth being adapted for rails. From 1,200 to 1,300 tons of plates can be made here weekly, while the production of rails varies from 600 to 800 tons per week. The company have a large continental and American connection; while their plates are known to, and more or less used by almost every shipbuilder in the British empire. The wages paid at Consett is something like £360,000 per annum, all told; and the value of the sales at the Co-operative Stores carried on in connection with the works is nearly £20,000 per annum. The Company own 1,500 workmen's cottages on their property, and the education of the rising generation has been provided for by the erection of schools capable of accommodating 1,300 to 1,400 children. The manufacture of coke is extensively carried on, near to the iron-works, the company having upwards of 560 coke ovens, from which they not only supply their own furnaces, but serve several works in the Cumberland district, and the locomotives on the Northern railways. The total output of coal from the company's collieries is about 12,000 tons per week. Taken as a whole, the Consett Company's Works are the largest in the North of England with perhaps three or at the most four exceptions.

When the proneness to take advantage of the Limited Liability Act was so rampant in 1866, a project was initiated for the amalgamation of the three important shipbuilding and engineering firms of Richardson, Denton, Duck, and Company, South Stockton; Denton, Grey, and Company, Hartlepool; and

Thomas Richardson and Sons, Hartlepool, under the designation of Richardsons, Denton, Duck, and Company. The object of this amalgamation was twofold. It was undertaken, in the first place, with a view to the more advantageous and extended working of the firms forming the triumvirate; and in the next place it was designed to take advantage of the Limited Liability Act. Mr. Dale was appointed vice-chairman of this huge undertaking, which, however, was not found to work so satisfactorily in combination as was expected; and it was, therefore, soon resolved into its original separate elements. In this connection it may be observed that, along with Mr. Robert Fletcher and Mr. Nicholson, of Manchester, Mr. Dale, who has had no previous connection with the concern, was elected one of the liquidators of that ill-started venture—Pile, Spence, and Company (Limited)—which, after giving promise of great things, and securing the confidence and means of hundreds of gullible shareholders, closed its career like a " flash in the pan," and involved many of its too confiding victims in absolute ruin. Among other local concerns with which Mr. Dale is identified, mention may be made of the Weardale and Shildon Water Works Company, of which he has been vice-chairman for several years. He is also associated with two or three smaller

concerns of an industrial character, either as
shareholder or director.

Since its formation in 1868, Mr. Dale has
acted as honorary treasurer of the Iron and
Steel Institute of Great Britain. At the
time of its formation he was one of its most
zealous advocates, and as a member of the
committee appointed under the resolution
that decreed its formation, he has done much
to make it a success, although we believe he
has not as yet contributed any papers to its
proceedings.

Under the Mines' Regulation Act of 1872,
a Board required to be created in each
mining inspection district, consisting of three
colliery owners, three colliery or mining engineers, and three workmen, along with the
Government Inspector. The duty of the
Board is to appoint examiners and to define
the subjects and character of the examination
for certificates entitling their holders to be
managers of collieries or mines under the Act,
which provides that every mine and colliery
must now be under the control of a certifica-
ted manager. When the Board for South
Durham and Cleveland was formed in the
early part of the present year, Mr. Dale was
at once appointed president,—a position
not more honourable than onerous in its
nature. A new motive power, no matter how
simple its mechanism may be, is generally

somewhat difficult to get into full and proper working order; but in this case the Board started on its career with the promise of a high degree of usefulness and efficiency, and without the operation of any disqualifications or trammels likely to interfere with the fulfilment of its high functions.

About four years ago Mr. Dale was appointed managing director of the Stockton and Darlington Railway. In our sketch of the late Mr. Joseph Pease, we spoke of the importance of this section, not only on its own merits, but as a feeder to the more comprehensive system of the North-Eastern Company, in which it is now absorbed. The traffic in minerals is larger than that of any other system of corresponding extent in the world; and the revenues of the company are proportionately great. But, more than this, the system is quite a monopoly throughout its entire length. Between Benfieldside and Saltburn-by-the-Sea—the two termini of the line—there is no alternative route. All the coal and coke from the South Durham coal-field, and all the limestone from Forcett, Stanhope, and other parts of Weardale is carried into the Cleveland district by this railway, while the great bulk of the iron and ironstone sent out of Cleveland must traverse the same route. In his management of the Darlington section, Mr. Dale has stuck pretty

closely to the somewhat hard and fast line
laid down by his predecessors. Its management is still a mild sort of despotism.
The austere and rigorous habits and principles of the communion that has so long
dominated over it may still be seen and felt.
The first passenger railway in England is
undoubtedly somewhat behind, or at any rate
out of harmony with the times. Querulous
travellers and "jolly good fellows" may
look hopefully forward to the time when
an administration shall arise that knows
not the Quakers—when · bitter beer and
brandy galore shall be accessible at every
refreshment room. After all, however, the
primary duty of a managing director is
towards the shareholders, and under Mr.
Dale, the dividends of the Stockton and
Darlington section have not come to grief.

Opinions may differ as to the principles which
govern the application of arbitration in
the settlement of trade disputes; but there
is no room for doubt as to the immense good
which the use of that system has effected in
the North of England. Arbitration is by no
means a new thing. Its merits and *rationale*
had been foreshadowed by speculative philos-
ophers long before its use was fairly resorted
to in this country. As a means of arranging
trade difficulties and disputes, it was first successfully applied by Mr. Mundella, M.P., to

M

the hosiery and other trades of Nottingham, and by Mr. Rupert Kettle, County Court Judge of Worcestershire, to the building trades of Wolverhampton. But the system was yet in its infancy when it was determined to apply it to the iron trade of the North of England. This was in the early part of 1869. The idea of setting up such a tribunal as a permanent mode of settling trade difficulties was first broached at a meeting of the North of England iron trade, the original suggestion emanating from Mr. Dale. On the first Monday in March, 1869, the Board was formally constituted. Its object was declared to be "to arbitrate on wages, or on any other matters affecting their respective interests that may be referred to it from time to time by either employers or operatives, by conciliatory means to interpose its influence to prevent disputes, and to put an end to any that may arise." The constitution of the Board provides that it shall be composed of one employer and one operative from each works joining it; and both employers and operatives must select their representatives at meetings to be held in December of each year. There is a standing committee consisting of four employers and four operatives, in addition to the president and vice-president, to which all questions are in the first instance referred for investigation. This committee endeavour to

settle matters coming before them, but have
no power to make any award. It was unanimously resolved that Mr. David Dale should
be appointed the first president of the Board,
the vice-president being chosen from among
and by the operatives. It would be. a mistake to say that since its establishment the
Board has worked with unvarying smoothness,
that it has realised all the expectations of its
promoters, or that it has prevented entirely
the occurrence of trade disputes. But it is
simple justice to say that its inauguration
ushered in a millennium of peace and goodwill
between employers and employed, compared
with the chaotic and demoralizing state of
matters that previously existed. In the iron
trade of the North of England, the principle
of arbitration found itself face to face with
elements that it had never before encountered.
There were many thousands of workmen
guided by and dependent upon its application.
Within a month after it was established it was
resolved to call in Mr. Rupert Kettle to determine a claim for increased wages upon
which the Board itself was unable to agree.
Mr. Kettle's decision was accepted as satisfactory, and after his award had been delivered
he was presented with a handsome testimonial. But when the next case of difference
arose, Mr. Thomas Hughes, the late member for
Frome, and the author of "Tom Brown's

School Days," was asked to undertake the duties of arbitrator. In his case, as in the case of Mr. Kettle, all the data necessary to lead to a just and sound conclusion were supplied. The employers produced their contract books and the terms of their specifications, while the workmen pointed to the wages paid in other districts, and furnished collateral arguments in support of their claim. The first awards of Mr. Hughes were satisfactory to both sides; but his last award was received by the workmen with intense dissatisfaction; and at the meeting at which it was announced, he was so roughly handled, and treated with so much disrespect, that he vowed he would never again undertake a similar duty. This is probably the ugliest phase of the Board's career. Although there have been occasional strikes at individual works, there never has, since a Court of Arbitration was established in the district, been a general and concerted strike. It is scarcely necessary to add that this happy change in the relations of employer and employed has been productive of equal benefit to both. The masters can now book contracts with the assurance that wages in certain departments will remain unaltered for a definite period, and that in these departments, also, there is no likelihood of anything occuring to disturb the even course

of his arrangements; while the workmen
have realised the unspeakable advantage of
regular wages without any serious breaks in
their time by circumstances within their own
control. Those of them who took part in the
great and desolating strike of 1866 will
fully appreciate the beneficent effects of the
change which the Court of Arbitration brought
about. Looking at it, indeed, from a purely
utlitarian and politico-economic point of view,
it must have saved many thousands of pounds
to the district; and from a humanitarian
aspect, it may be said to have achieved still
greater triumphs. It has put an end to the
" brutal arbitrament of the sword," and substituted in its stead the sober, rational, un-
impassioned judgment of impartial and un-
prejudiced men. It is true that arbitration
has not always and in all circumstances been
equally successful. It was attempted in
Scotland in 1870. when Mr. George Anderson,
M.P., was asked to decide on the disputed
claims of a large body of ironworkers; but
Mr. Anderson's award was such a prolific
source of discontent and rancour, that there
was another strike immediately on the back
of its publication; and many of those interested,
including both masters and workmen, have resolved to have nothing more to do with arbitration in the time to come. In South Staffordshire, on the other hand, a Court of

Conciliation has lately been established on a basis much resembling that on which the North of England Board is founded, and with highly successful results.

Much of the success of the Northern Board of Arbitration is due to the mingled tact, firmness, and discrimination of its president. Mr. David Dale is the possessor of an eminently judicial mind. He is also well versed in all the virtues of diplomacy—not a diplomacy of a mean, subservient, unconscionable kind—but of that loftier quality that discriminates between seemingly irreconcileable issues, and opens up a pathway to their perfect agreement. He is fertile in the suggestion of expedients, which remove many difficulties from the way of an amicable understanding between the rival interests represented at the Arbitration Board. But, above all, he preserves an unruffled temper; and through his equable behaviour, good humour is reflected upon his less self-controlled *collaborateurs* who would, probably, but for his influence, be prone to fall out by the way. In recognition of his valuable services to the Arbitration Board, Mr. Dale was in April, 1870, publicly presented with an address, subscribed by the representatives of every firm connected with the institution, in which the most flattering testimony was borne to his conduct of its proceedings.

Mr. Dale is a Justice of the Peace for the county of Durham, and is intimately mixed up with the various public, religious, political, educational, and benevolent institutions of the southern division of the county. On the death of the late Mr. Gurney Pease, he became a partner in the firm of Joseph Pease and Partners; and at the same time he was admitted into the firm of J. and J. W. Pease. In this capacity he is now one of the largest mineral owners in the North of England. He is married to the widow of the late Mr. H. Whitwell, C.E., by whom he has two children.

XII.—BERNHARD SAMUELSON, M.P.

Duʀing the last few years, a combination of causes, all more or less exceptional, has resulted in bringing the name of Mr. Bernhard Samuelson prominently before his countrymen at home and abroad. Not the least important of these has been his efforts on behalf of technical education. More than any man of his time he has become identified with this question. He has looked at it from all points of the mental compass. By his means its consideration has been forced upon the Government, and it is due to him that we now know, better than we ever did before, how we stand in the industrial balance as compared with Continental countries. In a letter addressed to the Vice-President of the Council, printed by order of the House of Commons in 1868, Mr. Samuelson clearly and ably pointed out the necessity of systematic technical instruction, in order to maintain and develope our national industries. We have, however, chiefly to speak of Mr. Samuelson

with regard to his long and important connection with Cleveland—a connection scarcely
less large and influential than that of any who·
have been associated with him in the same
sphere of enterprise.

Mr. Bernhard Samuelson was born on the
22nd day of November, 1820. His father
was a Liverpool merchant in a rather extensive
way of business. After being educated at a
private school, taught by the Rev. J. Blezards,
vicar of Skerlaugh, Yorkshire, young Bernhard entered a mercantile office in Liverpool,
where he was employed for six years. He
then went to the continent, where he was
engaged to look after the extensive contracts
in locomotive work of Messrs. Sharp, Stewart,
and Company of Manchester. His connection
with this well-known firm was both useful and
profitable, for he made the acquaintance of
some of the most eminent Continental
engineers, and the character of his avocations
demanded that he should be continually moving from place to place. In this way he saw
a great deal of Continental life, especially in
France and Germany, and he made the most
of his abundant opportunities for studying the
special merits and requirements of Continental
engineering. He was led also to engage in
some speculations of his own, which turned
out to be remunerative. Returning to England in his twenty-eighth year, he became the

purchaser of a small implement works and foundry at Banbury, where he took up his abode. Into this concern he threw his whole energies for a number of years, until he has made it famous all over the world. Samuelson's agricultural implements are perhaps as well known in Russia and Italy as they are among the farmers of Kent and Sussex. The firm have for many years done a very large export trade. In 1872 they turned out the enormous number of over 8,000 reaping-machines. Some kinds of implements are of Mr. Samuelson's own invention, and are made only at Banbury. Of course, the works have very largely increased in the hands of their present proprietor, until now they are probably the largest of their kind in England.

In the autumn of 1853, Mr. Samuelson attended the Cleveland Agricultural Society's Show, held that year at Stokesley, in order to exhibit a new digging-machine, which he had just patented. It was his first visit to Cleveland. Personally he knew nothing whatever of the district. The most he had heard of it was that it was a splendid field for agricultural operations, and he expected, doubtless, to do a good stroke of business among the farmers. He had heard also of John Vaughan, although he had never met him. As a gentleman indirectly concerned in the iron trade, he could not but be solicitous

to witness the results of Mr. Vaughan's
achievements. In common with many others
who were not near enough the root of the
prejudice to have their minds disabused, he
had been led to form anything but a favourable opinion as to the qualities of the Cleveland ironstone. The idea of becoming
more directly connected with the iron trade
had, however, long been in his thoughts,
and a fortuitous chain of events ultimately
led up to that result. He was introduced
to Mr. Vaughan by the late Mr. Dock-
ray, resident engineer of the London and
North-Eastern Railway, and Mr. Vaughan in
his usually open and communicative manner,
disclosed the position and prospects of the
district. He spoke of what had been done in
the way of opening up the Cleveland ironstone, the supplies of which he declared to be
illimitable. Mr. Samuelson had previously
visited the works at Eston, in the company of
Mr. T. Parrington, whose guest he was, and he
interpreted aright the merits of the situation.
He saw that in its most embryo state, the
district contained all the elements of prospective greatness. So thoroughly had he
become infected with Mr. Vaughan's spirit of
sanguine hope and confidence, that before he
left Cleveland he had concluded arrangements
for the purchase of a site at South Bank for
the erection of blast furnaces. This *locale* was

within a mile of the works of Messrs. Bolckow
and Vaughan at Eston, and it was agreed that
the latter firm should supply the South Bank
furnaces with ironstone from their Eston
mines. At that time the whole of the intervening space between Eston and the Middlesbrough Docks was almost a complete waste.
South Bank, where there is now a population
of some 4,000 or 5,000, was represented by one
or two small tumble-down farm steadings.
Elwon and Company had just commenced to
erect the Cleveland furnaces near by, and
there were incipient manifestations of industrial activity about the hamlet of Ormesby,
where Messrs. Cochrane and Company had
begun to erect four furnaces. Mr. Samuelson
decided on erecting three furnaces at South
Bank, each 50 feet in height, by 14 feet diameter at their boshes or widest part, and a
cubical capacity of 5,050 feet. He carried
on the Eston Works until the year 1863,
when he disposed of them to Major Elwon,
who subsequently sold them to Mr. Thomas
Vaughan. Under the ownership of the latter
gentleman the works have been so much extended that they are now among the largest
of their kind in the North of England.

Mr. Samuelson, did not however, abandon
his connection with the Cleveland district.
On the very day on which the sale of South
Bank Works to Major Elwon was concluded,

he commenced negotiations for the purchase of
a site, and erected four furnaces at Newport,
within a short distance of Middlesbrough.
These four furnaces were each 69 feet in
height and 20 feet diameter at their widest
part. Two years previously, Messrs. Bolckow and Vaughan had built at Middlesbrough
two furnaces 75 feet in height and 16 feet 6
inches in diameter. But Mr. Samuelson
was not fully persuaded of the advantages of a great height in the blast furnace.
He seemed to think that more sterling advantages would accrue from an increase of
cubical capacity. Accordingly we find that
he gave each of his furnaces a capacity of
15,500 cubic feet, or nearly 3,000 feet more
than the next largest furnaces at that time
built in Cleveland. Four years later—in
1868—he added another furnace to his Newport Works, and in 1870 he built three more
furnaces, making eight in all. Unitedly
these furnaces are equal to the production
of 2,500 to 3,000 tons of pig iron per week.
They are fitted up in the most modern style,
and with such a scrupulous regard to the fulfilment of every known economical condition
that in May, 1871, Mr. Samuelson deemed it
worth while to bring them under the notice
of the Institution of Civil Engineers. In the
course of his paper, Mr. Samuelson pointed
out that whereas in three furnaces erected

by him in 1854 for smelting the same ore, the quantity of fuel required to produce a single ton of pig iron varied from 30 to 40 cwts., and in five furnaces erected in 1863-8 from 23 to 24 cwts.; the coke consumed in the two new furnaces was only 20·35 cwts. He showed also that this great economy of fuel was due, first to greater capacity, augmented from 5,000 cubic feet in the earlier furnaces to 16,000 in those next erected, and to 30,000 cubic feet in the two furnaces built in 1870. In the next place, a saving of fuel was due to increased temperature at the tuyeres—the blast having been increased from 680° in the earlier to 1,100° in the latter furnaces; and, lastly, he attributed the economy gained to increased regularity in working, the result of improvements of construction, all aiming at the greatest attainable solidity and simplicity. The entire cost of erecting these two latter furnaces, with accessory appliances, was stated by Mr. Samuelson to be £53,331 4s. 4d., exclusive of the price of land.

The last and most important venture in which Mr. Samuelson embarked was the construction of the Britannia Ironworks, Middlesbrough, which were commenced in July, 1870. The site selected for these works was, up till that time, a waste marsh; and it had to be made available for the purposes of the

works by covering it with slag. We believe
the plant of these works—which are adapted
for the manufacture of all kinds of finished
iron—is the largest ever put down at one
time. Standing upon twenty acres of land,
the Britannia Works, as now in operation,
comprise two departments technically known
as the forge and the mill. The forge contains 120 puddling furnaces, and in the mill
there are twelve of Siemens' gas-heating furnaces, with the necessary apparatus for gen-
erating the gas. The machinery is of the
newest and most approved description, including a blooming mill on White's patent,
and Brown's patent rail mill. The forge is
capable of producing 1,200 to 1,400 tons per
week of puddled bars. Within the last two
years the Britannia Works have been transferred to a limited liability company, with an
ordinary share capital of £200,000 in 4,000
shares of £50 each, and we learn from the
prospectus that " the works are disposed of
in consequence of the desire of the principal
proprietor—Mr. Samuelson—to retire as opportunity offers from all business engagements requiring his personal attention."

His unsuccessful attempt to manufacture
steel from Cleveland iron is probably the
most interesting phase ,of Mr. Samuelson's
experience as an ironmaster. In the course
of his travels on the Continent Mr. Samuel-

son witnessed the operation of the Siemens-Martin patent for the manufacture of steel, and was much struck with its apparent simplicity and effectiveness. He could not see why the native iron of Cleveland should not be made into steel with as much ease as the Spiegeleisen of Germany, or the hematite ores of Cumberland and other districts. But in order to put his ideas to a practical test, he caused a quantity of iron made at the Newport Works from Cleveland ore to be sent over to France, and his engineer, Mr. Howson, crossed the Channel to superintend the experiments. The results were so successful as to convince him of the practicability of what had previously seemed to be impracticable. Early in 1869, therefore, he leased the North Yorkshire Ironworks at South Stockton, and at a great expenditure of labour and capital, adapted them for the manufacture of steel rails, angles, plates, and sheets, on the Siemens-Martin system. At the same time he made arrangements for producing steel ingots at the Newport ironworks, where experiments that were in the main successful had been previously carried out. The principle of the Siemens-Martin system may be briefly explained. It consists in melting the wrought iron in a bath of cast iron, whereby the excess of carbon in the cast iron is neutralised by the absence of it in the wrought iron. Chemically considered, the principle is sound, and should yield steel of a superior quality. Indeed, it is claimed for the Siemens-Martin patent that it yielded steel of an exceptionally uniform degree of hardness. To secure this result proofs were taken out of the furnace from time to time during the operation of melting, and the necessary degree of hardness was determined by the addition of an extra quantity of wrought or cast iron as the case required. In theory, nothing could be simpler than this *rationale*. But in practice it was hedged about by many difficulties that have proved up to the present time to be practically insurmountable. The Cleveland Ironmaster's position in this, as in other matters where he enters into competition with other districts, is necessarily controlled *ab initio* by the quality of his ironstone. Now, the ore of Cleveland is not adapted to the manufacture of steel. In order to convey to the mind of the reader a just conception of the difficulties in the way of Mr. Samuelson's venture, it may be well to furnish the composition of an ordinary specimen of blast furnace metal or pig iron from unmixed Cleveland ore. It is as follows :—

Essential Elements { Iron	=	90·96
Manganese (absent)..........	=	0·00
Carbon...............	=	0·65
Extraneous Element—Nitrogen..........	=	0·40

	Carbon in excess..............	=	3·30
	Oxygen	=	1·10
	Magnesium...................	=	0·09
Vitiating	Silicon.......................	=	1·85
Elements	Aluminum...................	=	0·10
	Calcium	=	0.07
	Sulphur	=	0.30
	Phosphorus..	=	1.19

100.000

It is obvious to the merest novice in chemical and metallurgical science that before good steel can be obtained, all the extraneous and vitiating elements shown in the above analysis must be expelled from the iron; while on the other hand the elements that are deficient must be made up to their due proportions. The excess of carbon beyond what is needed to constitute steel must be got rid of, leaving only a moiety of the original percentage behind. All the other vitiating elements must be entirely expelled before the iron-master can attain the end he has in view. This, it need not be added, is a very difficult task—so difficult indeed that science has not yet placed at the disposal of her disciples the resources necessary to its achievement. In the Siemens-Martin process, the action of the oxide was continued until all, or nearly all, the carbon had been removed, and it was not until then that the phosphorus was reduced to a sufficient proportion to fit the iron for subsequent use in the manufacture of steel. The

malleable iron was then fused with a carbon-
aceous iron free from phosphorus, such as
Swedish and hematite pig. But the results
were always indeterminate. Hence it followed,
that while at one time steel of an undoubtedly
excellent quality was obtained, the results
evolved at another time were unsatisfactory
in the highest degree. In the manufacture of
iron and steel, as much as in the manufacture
of any article of domestic use, there must be
certainty and regularity of results. An iron
or steel manufacturer never books a contract
but he is compelled to adhere to the most
rigorous specifications, the non-fulfilment of
which would involve the risk of having
thousands of tons rejected and thrown back
upon his hands. Under these circumstances
it will easily be understood that the Siemens-
Martin process could not be prosecuted with
any degree of satisfaction. Failing to see any
probability of reaching the goal in view, Mr.
Samuelson abandoned the venture after a
trial extending over many months. The
steel melting furnaces erected at Newport
were removed; and the North Yorkshire
works were entirely suspended; nor was
the latter establishment again re-opened
until it had been almost completely re-constructed under the auspices of the limited
liability company by whom it is now owned,
and of which Mr. Samuelson is a large shareholder.

Without a doubt this was one of the most dismal failures that ever took place in connection with the metallurgy of Cleveland. But it was not the only failure. Many of the Cleveland ironmasters had about that time and for some years previously, dabbled more or less in the same direction. Mr. Samuelson only carried out on a large scale and with buoyant confidence as to the results, that which his neighbours had now and again been tinkering at with fear and trembling. To Mr. Samuelson, therefore, belongs the credit of having given the experiment every justice ; and his failure in the long run was not a thing to be deprecated. It is only by repeated failures that some of the grandest discoveries of our time have been arrived at. Stephenson, Watt, Arkwright, Newton, and Bessemer—all the men, in short, who have benefitted the world by their inventions and discoveries, while building princely fortunes for themselves— have achieved ultimate success not because but in spite of repeated failures. In Mr. Samuelson's case there was no idea of "wading through dirt to dignity." He went into the speculation thoroughly, determined to spend and to be spent in order to accomplish his end. As it was, it involved a loss of something like £25,000 or £30,000. But had it turned out a genuine success, it would have secured for Cleveland the one thing needful to give it pre-eminence over all other districts in metallurgical science. Cleveland steel from Cleveland iron would have defied competition. It would have been produced much cheaper than steel is now produced from the expensive ores used in its manufacture. Whether the end for which Mr. Samuelson laboured will ever be attained remains an inscrutable problem; but the hon. gentleman will always take rank as one who exerted himself to bring about its solution.

No sketch of Mr. Samuelson would be complete if it failed to register his efforts on behalf of technical education. In the autumn of 1867, the honourable member visited France, Belgium, Germany, and Switzerland, for the purpose of obtaining accurate information as to their industrial position—more especially as to their recent manufacturing, progress, and the state of labour and instruction among them. His mission was undertaken entirely on his own responsibility, but he had the co-operation of the Education Department of the Privy Council and of the Secretary for Foreign Affairs, by whom he was furnished with credentials recommending him to the assistance and good offices of Her Majesty's foreign consuls. Before proceeding to the Continent, the honourable gentleman made a tour of the principal manufacturing centres of England, visiting the principal works in Cleveland, South Durham,

Lancashire, Yorkshire, and Nottinghamshire. He was thus placed in a position to compare the relative positions of our own and other countries, and he elicited the views of our own and foreign manufacturers, which materially assisted him in forming his conclusions. On the last Saturday of 1867, after his return from his self-imposed task, Mr. Samuelson issued a circular to the Vice-President of the Committee of Council on Education, in which he stated at length the results of his observations. On the whole, he did not think the Continent was much, if at all, ahead of England in the matter of industrial progress and attainments. He found that in various mechanical manufactures improvements which had originated in Cleveland had been adopted on the Continent, and in the construction of engines and machinery, Belgium, France, and Germany were following in the footsteps of Great Britain. But while he considered that foremen, managers, and proprietors generally were better educated on the Continent than in England, he could not say so much for the workmen. One important point to which Mr. Samuelson called attention was the facilities afforded on the Continent for the carriage of minerals. Ores were carried in France at rates below three-eighths of a penny per ton per mile, and coal was sent from Westphalia to France, Holland, and Germany, at one half-

penny per ton per mile, including the use of
the wagons. These rates, we need not add,
are much below those that are levied in the
North of England.

The effects of Mr. Samuelson's disclosures,
and the recommendations he made for the
improvement of technical education in this
country, need hardly be stated here at any
length. On the motion of the honourable
member, the House of Commons appointed
a committee to inquire into the whole subject of technical education; and in this and
other ways the question was thoroughly ventilated. The interest evoked by Mr. Samuelson's letters and speeches—for he addressed
public meetings on the subject in many of
the principal towns in England—had scarcely
subsided, when the question was again re-
vived by Mr. Plimsoll, M.P. for Derby, who
wrote to the *Times* several letters, in which
he went thoroughly into the competition
between England and Belgium as regards
the manufacture of iron. Mr. Plimsoll had
gone scientifically into the subject, and
showed exactly how, when, and where the
Belgian manufacturers economised fuel which
in England was completely wasted. Mr.
Isaac Lowthian Bell, at a meeting of the
North of England Ironmasters' Association
held in 1868, read a paper on the same vexed
question, which was largely at that time the

question of the day. The last three or four years, however, have done much to allay the somewhat alarmist views promulgated through Mr. Plimsoll and others who shared his views, as opposed to those of Mr. Samuelson, while within the same time, and probably as the result of the labours of these gentlemen, increased attention has been given to the technical education of all who are interested in our staple manufactures, both from the State and from more private sources.

Mr. Samuelson has taken a high and influential position as a representive of the industrial interests in the House of Commons. His evidence and opinions on questions of commercial import have been called for over and over again. In the sessions of 1871 and 1872 he was chairman of the committee appointed to inquire into the subject of letters patent—a question in which he had himself for years previously taken a prominent interest. Before that committee some valuable evidence was tendered by such men as Henry Bessemer, M. Schnieder, of the great Cruezot Works, Isaac Holden, and Sir Roundell Palmer. The general tenor of the evidence showed that the patent laws of this country were sadly in want of amendment; that about 3,000 or more patents are taken out yearly, and of this number no more than 500 are proceeded with after the lapse of three years,

during which provisional protection is usually
allowed. The deliberations of the Patent
Committee were studied with great avidity
by the scientfic public, and the recommendations which they made are likely to place
the system of the patent laws on a much
more equitable and satisfactory footing.

During the last ten or fifteen years Mr.
Samuelson has taken an active part in the
public affairs of Cleveland. Although residing permanently at Banbury, he has frequently
found time and opportunity to run down to
Middlesbrough, where he has stayed sometimes for weeks together. He has thus
become identified with several of the local
institutions of Cleveland. He is a member
of the Cleveland Institution of Engineers, of
the North of England Ironmasters' Association, and of the Middlesbrough Chamber of
Commerce. He is at the present time President of the Cleveland Literary and Philoso-
phical Society, and from time to time he has
contributed liberally to local charities and
other institutions.

In 1844, Mr. Samuelson married Caroline,
daughter of Mr. Henry Blundell, a Hull merchant. In politics he is a Liberal. First
elected for Banbury in February, 1859, he
was rejected at the election in April of that
year. In July, 1865, he again offered himself as a candidate and was accepted. Since

then he has sat continuously for Banbury, while his son, who was elected member for Cheltenham in 1868, has also found a seat in the House of Commons.

XIII.—CHARLES MARK PALMER, M.P.

Little need be said to justify the inclusion in the present series of articles of the name of Mr. Charles Mark Palmer. If not so immediately connected as some of his contemporaries with the earlier development of the Cleveland iron trade, he has done much to promote its exuberant growth, in all its various ramifications; and throughout the whole of his long business career he has displayed an amount of energy, foresight, and enterprise that can scarcely be paralleled in the industrial annals of the North of England. To him it is greatly if not mainly due that the Tyne has taken a leading position as a mart of naval architecture. The renown of Palmer's shipbuilding works is more than merely local. It has spread to the remotest corners of the earth, fostering and maintaining as much as the Lairds of Birkenhead or the Napiers of Glasgow the prestige of Great Britain as the greatest naval power in Europe. Nor is it in naval architecture alone that the well-known Jarrow firm have won their laurels. They occupy a position scarcely subordinate to any held in the North of England as mineral owners and iron manufacturers. Unlike the Birtley, the Lemington, and other works that have been overtaken by vicissitudes to which they were ultimately compelled to succumb, the works of Jarrow have been carried on continuously and successfully since they had a beginning, no efforts having been spared to keep pace with the genius of improvement, and harmonise with the altered circumstances induced by new discoveries and applications of mechanical, metallurgical, and chemical science.

Born in King Street, South Shields, in 1822, Mr. Charles Mark Palmer is now in the fifty-first year of his age. His father, who will still be well-remembered in Tyneside, was the owner of a Greenland whaler, for a number of years. Subsequently, he engaged in the Indian trade, for which he first chartered and then acquired vessels that sailed from the Tyne. After receiving the rudiments of his education in South Shields, young Charles was sent to Bruce's Academy, Percy Street, Newcastle, which was then esteemed one of the first educational seminaries in the " canny toon," and from thence he proceeded for a short time to the south of France, where he completed his studies. Commencing his business career in the office of Messrs. Palmer Beckwith and Company, timber merchants, in which his father was a partner, he soon found what promised to be a more lucrative enterprise, in the manufacture of coke, upon which he embarked at Marley Hill, with Sir William Hutt, the late Mr. Nicholas Wood, and Mr. John Bowes as his partners. Contact and association with such men sharpened the natural aptitude for commercial success possessed by Mr. Palmer; and he became within twelvemonths a partner in the Marley Colliery along with the gentlemen already named. This was in the year 1845, and two years later we find Mr. Palmer and his partners acquiring collieries belonging to Lorn Ravensworth. From this date, he was enabled to go on " prospering and to prosper," adding every year to the number of his achievements and the extent of his possessions.

About the year 1850, the heavy expense and inconvenience attending the carriage of coal by railway began to affect seriously the sale of north country coal in the London market. Durham and Northumberland coalowners found that they had no longer the monopoly that was formerly theirs, for new fields were being developed in various parts of the kingdom that had more easy and economical access to the London market. To

compensate for the disadvantages under which
the northern coal owners laboured in regard
to facilities for transport and distance, and to
prevent the loss of the sceptre which they
had wielded so long, Mr. Palmer constructed
a screw collier, built to carry 650 tons, and
to steam about nine miles an hour. The success of the experiment was not immediate.
It was to some extent one of those " inventions born before their time," which, according to the late Emperor Napoleon, " must
remain useless until the level of the common
intellect rises to comprehend them." Not
that the invention was premature with respect to its necessity—very few inventions
are ; but under the then imperfect conditions
of nautical knowledge it encountered an
amount of prejudice and opposition that
would not be likely to arise at this time of
day. It was argued that it would be impossible for steamers carrying 650 tons of coal,
and costing about £10,000, to compete with
sailing crafts that consumed no fuel, and
which, although only carrying one-half the
burden cost little more than £1000, or only
about one-tenth the amount. But it was the
old story over again. In a contest of steam
against wind, the latter power must go the
wall. Certitude, regularity, and speed enabled the steam collier to achieve an ultimate
triumph ; and after the success of the first

screw collier had been clearly demonstrated, Mr. Palmer organised the Screw Collier Company, of which for a number of years he was both adviser and director. It may be interesting to mention that on her first voyage, the John Bowes—the initial screw collier— was laden with 650 tons of coals in four hours; in forty-eight hours she arrived in London ; twenty-four hours she discharged her cargo ; and in forty-eight hours more she was again in the Tyne ; so that, as Mr. Palmer himself has put it, " in five days she performed, successfully, an amount of work that would have taken two average sized colliers upwards of a month to accomplish." The success of Mr. Palmer's experiment completely revolutionised the coal carrying trade of the Tyne. In 1852 when the first screw collier commenced to ply, there were only seventeen cargoes, representing 9,483 tons of coal, imported into London by screw-steamers; but within ten years (in 1862), there were no less than 1,427 cargoes so imported, making a total of 929,825 tons of coal, and in 1869 the number of cargoes carried by iron screw colliers, to and from London, had increased to 2,440, and 1,716,563 tons of coal. Since 1852, the screw collier has undergone several important improvements, in the carrying out of which Mr. Palmer has lent his valuable assistance, and as illustrating the measure of progress made, it may be stated that the James Dixon made fifty-seven voyages to London in one year, delivering 62,842 tons of coal, with a crew of only twenty-one persons. It is calculated that this work could only have been accomplished under the old system of sailing colliers with sixteen ships and 114 hands to man them. But in seeking to stimulate the London coal trade, Mr. Palmer did not confine his attention and exertions to the construction of steam colliers. He devised hydraulic machinery for enabling them to unload expeditiously and without trouble; and to complete the facilities necessary to the end he had in view—that, namely, of keeping the London trade in the hands of the northern coal masters—he leased the North London Railway for the purpose of systematically and easily throwing the cargoes into all parts of the metropolis. It is unnecessary to add that the northern coal owners were by these and other means enabled to maintain their supremacy, and that they still continue to hold their own in the markets of the world.

It was in the year 1852 that Mr. Charles M. Palmer, conjointly with his brother George, commenced shipbuilding at Jarrow, a place hallowed by the memory of the Venerable Bede. At that time it was only a small village, its population not exceeding 1,000 inhabitants. Now, thanks mainly to the

enterprise of the Messrs. Palmer, it has a
community of over 22,000 souls. Until 1857
the Messrs. Palmer confined their operations
to marine architecture, including, of course,
the construction of their own engines. But
in that year they added four blast furnaces,
and a year later, in 1859, they built rolling
mills. Simultaneously with these extensions
the firm acquired a lease of ironstone royalties
at Staithes, midway between Saltburn and
Whitby. No attempt had then been made to
open out the ironstone in this part of Cleveland. The district was a real *terra incognito*.
It could hardly be approached directly from
any side. The nearest railway terminus was
Saltburn, distant nine or ten miles, and the
sea could not conveniently be used as a highway from the absence of harbour accommodation. The first thing, therefore, that the
Messrs. Palmer did was to construct a harbour
at Port Mulgrave, where their vessels could
be provided with safe anchorage while receiving their cargoes. This undertaking involved an outlay of some £40,000 to £50,000.
When the mines were opened out, the Messrs.
Palmer commenced to run a fleet of steamers
for the removal of the ironstone. These
vessels carried cargoes of coal to London, and
called at Port Mulgrave to ship the ironstone
on their return voyage. The quantity of ironstone brought to the Jarrow furnaces is from

P

2,500 to 3,000 tons per week. Two separate beds of stone are worked at the Port Mulgrave mines. The top bed is four feet in thickness, the lower bed is 8 feet thick, and between the two there are 200 feet of intervening strata, principally composed of alum shale.

It is not within the purpose of this article to furnish a detailed description of the Jarrow works. Briefly it may be said that they comprise six departments, divided thus—

I.—The ironstone mines.

II.—The blast furnace department, in which the manufacture of pig iron, kentledge, and rough castings of every kind is carried on.

III.—The forges and rolling mills, producing angle iron of all sizes, up to 10 and 3 inches; rounds and squares up to 5 inches; bulb iron up to 10 inches deep; merchant bars, rails, and plates of all sorts and sizes.

IV.—The engine works, where marine and land engines, boilers, forgings, iron and brass castings, and general machinery are made.

V.—The iron shipyard and graving docks at Jarrow.

VI.—The bridge building yard at Howden, where every description of bridge building work is carried on.

It will thus be seen that the firm possess within themselves everything that they require for the purpose of their huge business.

It is quite within the record to affirm that there is not a more complete and independent establishment in the world. Extracting the ores from the bowels of the earth, they carry it up through all intervening processes, until it is turned out in the form of stately merchantmen, fitted up with a luxuriousness and taste that rivals the splendour and comfort of Belgravian drawing rooms; or, it may be that it takes the form of a marine armament, qualified, from its invulnerable power and death-dealing properties, to maintain the unrivalled reputation of Great Britain as mistress of the seas; or, again, it is transformed into the most subtle and complicated machinery, used for the multiform purposes embraced within the ample limits of the industrial arts. This huge concatenation of resources owes its existence and rare excellence of combination to the constructive genius and administrative capacity of Charles Mark Palmer. It was he who presided at the helm of affairs when the colossal fabric was being raised; and it was he who, while "its greatness was a ripening," controlled, down to the utmost trifling minutiæ, the whole course of events. In 1865 Mr. Palmer built a graving dock— still, we believe, the largest on the north-east coast, which is 440 feet in length, and has a depth of 18 feet of water at ordinary spring tides. The Jarrow establishment not only embraces the manufacture of iron in all its various forms and combinations; but it employs the services of a whole army of artizans—plumbers, glaziers, painters, sailmakers, rivetters, joiners, upholsterers, and, in brief, representatives of every trade that has the remotest connection with the construction or equipment of iron ships. On the west side of the furnaces, gasworks have been erected, capable of supplying 2,500.000 cubic feet of gas per month, which is distributed throughout the works. Reliable returns of the result of the year 1872 enables us to form a definite estimate of the enormous resources of the Jarrow works. The total quantity of ironstone smelted was 156,000 tons, producing 87,600 tons of pig iron. The tonnage of the ships launched was 11,500 tons, their horsepower being 2,500 nominal, while near 50,000 tons of plates and bars were manufactured. Throughout the whole establishment the total quantity of coal consumed, including the coke used in the blast furnaces, is little short of half a million tons per annum.

In 1862, Mr. George Palmer retired from the business, and Mr. C. M. Palmer carried it on alone until 1866, when it was transferred to a limited liability company. Mr. Palmer, however, continued to retain a large interest in the concern, and has acted as chairman since the formation of the company. Although subject to the fluctuations and vicissitudes that attend the conduct of all large commercial undertakings, Palmer's Iron Ship-building Company has enjoyed a large amount of prosperity under the new administration; its revenues have not fallen off, nor has the lustre of its name been tarnished.

It now becomes our province to speak more particularly of that department which forms Mr. Palmer's proudest and most conspicuous title to the exceptional position he occupies among the merchant princes of the British Empire. It should be remembered that Mr. Palmer was something more than a mere naval builder and architect, he was also a great projector and organizer. He took a prominent part in the establishment of the National Line, which now carries on a large business between this country and the United States; and he has built many of the most splendid vessels owned by that Company. In 1861, he entered into a contract with the Italian Government to construct and work a line of steamers for the conveyance of the mails between the Italian Peninsula and Alexandria. He was further concerned in the promotion of the Guion line of Transatlantic mail steamers, all of which have been built at the Jarrow shipbuilding yard. When the extensive business carried on by Messrs. Ormston, Dobson, and Company, of the Antwerp and Dunkirk

Steam Shipping Company, as carriers of passengers and goods between the Tyne and Hamburg, Rotterdam, Antwerp, and Dunkirk, and that of Mr. W. D. Stephens, whose fleet of steamboats plied between Newcastle and London, were transferred to a limited liability company in 1864, the conduct of negotiations was left in the hands of Mr. Palmer, who carried them to a successful issue, and who was very appropriately elected chairman of the new proprietary, which has since traded under the name of the Tyne Steam Shipping Company. In a more national aspect, Mr. Palmer has acquired celebrity on account of the numerous war vessels which he has built for her Majesty's and other Governments. The first contract of this character entrusted to his execution by the British Government was the "Terror," one of the large iron-cased floating batteries designed during the Russian war to co-operate against Cronstadt. A proof of the great capabilities of the Jarrow Works is afforded by the fact that this vessel, of 2,000 tons, 250 horse-power, and carrying twenty-six 68-pounder guns, was built in three and a half months! Mr. Palmer himself declared that she would have been completed in three months, had not the declaration of peace slackened the energies of the workmen. In the construction of the "Terror," rolled armour plates were used for the first

time. Up to that period the demand for
forged armour plates was so great that the
forges of the kingdom could not supply it, and
the use of rolled plates was thus rendered
unavoidable. But the Admiralty, with its
usually perverse and short-sighted instincts,
opposed the substitution determined on by
Mr. Palmer, and the only course left open to
him was, therefore, that of proving their
efficiency and justifying his preference. The
Admiralty was invited to witness a trial of
rolled armour plates on a target bolted on to
the side of an old wooden frigate at Ports-
mouth. The result showed that while the
hammered plate split and cracked to pieces,
the rolled plates were only indented. To
quote Mr. Palmer's own words:—" A shot
was then tried to test the resisting power of
the compressed cotton, and it appeared to
answer so well that Captain Hewlett advised
a series of experiments to be tried. The
Admiralty were willing, but requested us to
provide the targets at our own expense.
Having already spent upwards of £1,500 on
experiments for the good of the country, we
declined this proposal; nevertheless, we had
proved to the Admiralty the important fact
that the rolled plates were superior to the
forged, and they have since been universally
adopted. We, therefore, claim for this

district the honour of being the first to prove the strength and utility of rolled armour plates, since known and spoken of in Parliament as ' Palmer's Rolled Plates.' "

To give anything like an exhaustive idea of the progress of the Jarrow establishment in the art of marine architecture would require the compass of a large volume. We can only glance at the broad and general results. From the commencement of shipbuilding operations in 1852 to the end of 1868, there had been launched at these works 239 vessels, of an aggregate burthen of 205,419 tons. Up to the end of 1872, the total number of vessels launched was over 260, and the aggregate burthen was about 250,000 tons, the engines made for the same period representing upwards of 30,000 horse-power. Besides the " Terror," already named, the firm have built the " Defence," an iron-plated frigate of 3,688 tons; the "Jumma," a troop ship of 4,173 tons ; the " Cerberus," which was fitted up to guard Melbourne harbour; the "Swiftsure," an iron-clad of 3,892 tons ; and the " Triumph," which was launched in presence of many members of the Social Science Congress on the occasion of the visit of that association to Newcastle, and was christened by the Duchess of Northumberland. All these war ships were built to the order of the British Government, thus proving the high estimation in which the capacity of the Jarrow Shipbuilding Company is held by the Admiralty.

Referring more particularly to the personal history of Mr. Palmer, it may be remarked that he has contributed many papers to the proceedings of scientific and technical societies. Being regarded as one of the greatest authorities of the day on all that relates to marine architecture, his prelections have a weight and influence that are claimed on behalf of very few of his contemporaries. At the Newcastle meeting of the British Association in 1863, he read a paper " On the construction of iron ships and the progress of shipbuilding operations on the Tyne, Wear, and Tees;" and at the May meeting of the Iron and Steel Institute of Great Britain—of which he is a member—in 1870, he read another valuable paper on "Iron as a material for shipbuilding, and its influence on the commerce and armament of nations." In concluding this paper, he observed that " we have in a great measure substituted iron for wood—we must now change iron for steel ;" and he suggested the desirability of devising methods of cheapening and rendering practicable the use of steel in ship construction. When the Institution of Mechanical Engineers visited Newcastle in 1869, they were privileged to inspect the Jarrow Shipbuilding Works,

Mr. Palmer himself acting as their cicerone. A luncheon was provided, at which several compliments were exchanged, and Mr. Palmer, in proposing "Success to the Institution of Mechanical Engineers," took occasion to say, that when the Society visited the North eleven years ago Jarrow was only a small village, although now, he added, "he was proud to think that Jarrow stood second to no other manufacturing locality on the banks of the Tyne. Every square yard along the busy banks of that river proved what mechanical engineers had accomplished. By their progressive intelligence and mechanical contrivances England must ever continue the greatest seat of manufacture in the world." Mr. Palmer has for many years been connected with the North of England Institute of Mining and Mechanical Engineers, and other technical societies. At the present time he is chairman of the local Shipbuilders' Association.

Besides the works at Jarrow, Mr. Palmer is largely interested in other commercial and industrial undertakings, including the Bede Metal Extracting Company, established at Jarrow some two or three years ago, and the Tyne Plate Glass Company. He is head of the firm of Messrs. Palmer, Hall, and Company, who have an extensive connection as shipowners, brokers, and general merchants in Newcastle and elsewhere. Among the honorary appointments which he holds, the chief are those of lieutenant-colonel of volunteers, and magistrate for the county of Durham and the North Riding of Yorkshire. In the general election of 1868 Mr. Palmer was an unsuccessful candidate for the representation of South Shields, in opposition to Mr. Stevenson. In 1874, however, he became a candidate for the representation of North Durham, conjointly with Mr. I. L. Bell, and after a severe contest, both of these gentlemen were returned in the Liberal interest to the new House of Commons. But their victory was not a long one. A petition was presented against their return, the hearing of which led to both being unseated, without, however, being disqualified from standing again. A new election, in June, 1874, placed Mr. Palmer at the head of the poll, and Sir George Elliot (Conservative) second, thus bringing about the defeat of Mr. Palmer's former colleague. A second petition was lodged against Mr. Palmer's return, but at the last moment it was withdrawn by its promoters, on the ground of insufficient evidence ; and the hon. gentleman still continues, therefore, in the position of senior member for North Durham.

Mr. Palmer has been twice married. By his first wife, who died in 1865, he has three sons, and by his second wife, he has also a family. He is owner of the Easington and Hinderwell manors, and of the Grinkle Park and Seaton Hall estates. He has done much to improve, not only the condition of these estates, but also the social well-being of his tenants, especially so far as providing educational facilities is concerned.

XIV.—JOHN GJERS.

The story of the life of Mr. John Gjers introduces us to the purely technical, or, in other words, to the engineering phase of the progress of the Cleveland Iron Trade. There is no aspect of metallurgy more important than that which belongs to the province of the engineer. It is his business to provide improved methods and processes, to adapt machinery to special circumstances and peculiar cases, to devise ways and means of economy previously unknown, and in a word, to maintain our industrial pre-eminence. Without, therefore, undervaluing the indisputable necessity and importance of those functions that belong to chemistry on the one hand, and to geology on the other, we may fairly claim that the industrial arts owe at least as much to engineering as to either of these two sciences. This is especially true of Cleveland, where so . many engineering triumphs have been achieved; and seeing that no one has done more than Mr. Gjers to promote the interests of the district from an engineering point of view, it falls distinctly within the scope of our purpose to trace here the lines of his biography.

Born in Gothenburg, the second city of Sweden, Mr. Gjers comes of an old and highly respected family. He was brought up to the engineering profession in his native city, where he was afforded ample opportunities for combining the practice of his art with its scientific principles. In 1851, on the occasion of the first international exhibition held in this country, Mr. Gjers came over to England, and seeing that there was more scope for the practice of his profession than there was in his own country, he elected to take up his residence here. The three subsequent years he spent as an engineering draughtsman in various parts of Lancashire and Yorkshire; and in 1854 he came down to Middlesbrough to undertake a responsible position at the Ormesby Works. At Ormesby, he assisted Mr. Edwin Jones (now of the firm of Jones, Dunning, and Company), to build the original Ormesby blast furnaces; and his services were called into requisition by Mr. Henry Cochrane, who was then building the large pipe foundry at Ormesby. At the time of its completion, this was the largest foundry of its kind in Great Britain. It turned out 600 tons of castings per week; and it is no small compliment to the capacity of Mr. Gjers that, although he was then only twenty-four years of age, he was entrusted with the designs of all the machinery required for this large establishment. Mr. Edwin Jones retired from the management of the Ormesby Works in 1855, and Mr. Gjers became his successor. Until the year 1861, the latter continued to manage the blast furnace department. During this period those two great improvements in the economical production of pig iron—the introduction of a hotter blast and the successful utilization of the waste furnace gases for the raising of steam and the heating of the blast—were effected. At the Ormesby Works, Mr. Gjers took an active and prominent part in the carrying out of these improvements. By the former he was enabled to save from 7 to 8 cwt. of coke per ton of iron smelted, while the latter resulted in an economy of 10 to 12 cwt. of coal for every ton of pig iron produced.

It was under the superintendence of Mr. Gjers that the first of Siemen's and Cowper's newly patented heating stoves were introduced into the Cleveland district. This was in 1858. Mr. Gjers did not, however, go into this matter of his own accord. It is to Mr. Charles Cochrane that the application of these stoves to the Ormesby furnaces are entirely due. They were then very crude and complicated in design and action, and Mr. Gjers was so impressed with their imperfections (and their better performances in later years have not altogether removed his first impressions) that he ultimately resigned the management of the Ormesby Works. This he did without any unpleasantness on either side. He found that Mr. Charles Cochrane and himself could not pull together in the difficulties and expenses which arose out of the structural alterations proposed by the former, and rather than go on in a half-hearted way with undertakings of which he did not approve, he determined to abnegate his managerial functions altogether. A presentation made to him on the occasion of his departure, showed Mr. Gjers that he carried away with him the respect of his Ormesby co-workers.

It was during his connection with the Ormesby Works that Mr. Gjers patented his invention for superheating the blast and for heated air engines. Various contrivances had been designed for this purpose; but the gas-burner for stoves and boilers, patented and first applied by Mr. Gjers to No. 1 furnace at Ormesby, is now almost universally used in the Cleveland district.

In the beginning of 1862, Mr. Gjers was appointed manager for Messrs. Hopkins and Company, at the Teeside Ironworks. There were then only two furnaces in operation at this establishment. For a couple of years Mr. Gjers carefully superintended the operation of these furnaces, with a view to further improvements. Meanwhile, he had taken out a patent for granulating blast furnace slag by running it into agitated water in a fluid state. The resulting slag, in its granulated form, was used instead of sand to run pig iron into, for the purpose of moulding it as it came from the blast furnace. Very recently the same mode of granulating slag has been re-patented with another object in view; but as it was not found advantageous from an economical standpoint, Mr. Gjers allowed his patent to lapse.

In 1862, the question of obtaining a better fettling for puddling furnaces was exercising the minds of the iron masters of the North of England. Mr. Gjers conceived the idea of using rich magnetic ore for fettling purposes, and proved that by the substitution of such ores for those then in ordinary use, a great improvement could be effected in the quality of the iron, besides bringing out a greater weight of puddled bar than the weight of pig iron put into the furnace through the reduction of part of the fettling. Although very little attention was paid at the time to this formulæ, its correctness has since been proved by the use of the same class of ores, for the same purpose, in the Danks' puddling furnace, where the action of the fettling is more perfect.

Q

In the year 1864, the partners of the firm of Hopkins and Company decided to erect a new blast furnace plant adjacent to the Tees-side Works. The designing and carrying out of this new establishment was entrusted to Mr. Gjers. About that time more decided advances began to be made in the way of enlarging the size of the blast furnaces of Cleveland. There was, however, no experience to guide the iron master in determining the most advantageous limit of height and capacity. With characteristic caution, Mr. Gjers determined to erect the furnaces, which have since been named the Linthorpe Ironworks, on a medium scale. These works, however, mark an era when greatly improved furnaces began to be built in Cleveland, and they bear witness to the enterprise of their owners, who, in carrying them out, adopted a number of new arrangements proposed and designed by Mr. Gjers. Each of these arrangements are so important as to merit a special paragraph for itself.

From a purely mechanical point of view, the first and most important novelty of the Linthorpe Works was the new blowing-engines designed by Mr. Gjers. They are four direct acting non-condensing, overhead cylinder engines, with 30-inch steam cylinder, 66-inch blowing cylinders, and 4ft. stroke, each engine working singly, and at 32 revolutions per minute, a speed which is increased to 42

revolutions when one engine is laid off and
the remaining three blow four furnaces.
Their most interesting feature is the air
valves. These are simply flaps of Warne's
India-rubber. Each valve seat is a casting,
perhaps 30-inches long, with a number of
posts in the length, each three or four inches
long and $\frac{3}{4}$-inch or more wide, the posts being
separated by narrow bars, and the whole forming a grid. A flap of rubber $\frac{1}{4}$-inch thick
is fastened to one edge of the planed face of
the casting, and has a light plate-iron stop at
its back, allowing the flap to open through
about 30 deg. The blowing cylinder is made
to receive the required number of these valves
around its upper and lower ends, the valves
being set to act as inlets or outlets, as required.
About these valves there is no leakage of blast
and no noise, so that they appear to be the
best that can be devised. It is a proof of the
excellent working results of these engines,
that Messrs. Cochrane have since built at their
Ormesby Works two of the same general construction.

Another speciality of the Linthorpe Works,
is the pneumatic hoists or lifts, associated
with the name of Mr. Gjers, which were
erected here for the first time. These hoists
have been pronounced by competent authorities to be the best in the Cleveland
district, although they are rivalled by the

hydraulic hoist of Sir William Armstrong, the ordinary water balance hoist, the hydropneumatic hoist, in which compressed air is the medium accumulated, the direct acting steam ram lift, and the ordinary winding engine with drum and wire rope and reversing motion applicable to both vertical and inclined lifts. The pneumatic lift of Mr. Gjers is an exceedingly ingenious arrangement, applicable either to blast furnace or to calcining kilns, and it has now been adopted by several of the principal firms in the Cleveland district.

A new description of calcining kiln, and an entirely new type of heating stove, were also initiated by Mr. Gjers at the Linthorpe Ironworks. All of these inventions have become more or less common in the Cleveland district and elsewhere. At the Linthorpe Works, the whole of Mr. Gjers' new designs were found from the first to contain elements of superiority. Practical engineers and ironmasters scanned their operation with eager interest. They were more than satisfied with the result. Mr. Gjers made his name known far and near as one of the first blast furnace engineers of the day, and from that time forward his spurs were won.

1866, Messrs. Hopkins, Gilkes and Company, decided to erect a new blast furnace plant, and Mr. Gjers was entrusted with the prepar-

ation of the plans. In the following year the
new blast furnaces were blown in successfully,
and Mr. Gjers was complimented on the very
efficient manner in which he had performed
his work. A year later, and two more
furnaces of a still larger size were added to
the Linthorpe Ironworks. The latter furnaces were put into blast towards the close of
June, 1870, and the ceremony was attended
with more than usual *éclat*. A banquet, at
which most of the ironmasters of the district
were present, was given in celebration of the
event, and Mr. Thomas Vaughan, in proposing the health of the engineer of the works
—Mr. Gjers—said that "they ought to be
proud of a man who possessed such rare engineering ability."

No one has done more than the subject of
these remarks to solve the problem of making
Cleveland steel. In 1868, he took out a
patent for a new process, discovered after
many experiments, for the manufacture of
steel rails from the iron of the district, and
although the process was successful to the
extent of yielding the article desiderated, its
cost rendered its commercial success doubtful.
The *rationale* of the process may be briefly
explained. It consisted in boiling the iron in
a puddling furnace wrought with an extra
high heat, and fettled with rich oxide of iron.
By means of good stirring, the phosphorus

which had hitherto defied all attempts at complete elimination, was reduced to the merest trace, retaining about 1 per cent. of carbon, but before the iron began to "come to nature," as it is technically called, it was tapped into the open heart of a steel furnace (a Siemens' or any other furnace capable of giving sufficient heat to smelt steel being suitable for this purpose) where the decarbonization was completed by exposure until the metal reached the required consistency. It seems to be admitted on all hands that if the phosphorus could be eliminated from Cleveland iron, the other vitiating elements could be so far got rid of that it would be comparatively an easy matter to produce steel; but of nearly a dozen processes tried at one time or another, not one has yet achieved this primary result.

During the years under review, Mr. Gjers undertook the designing and carrying out of several important ironworks outside the Cleveland district. In 1867, a number of Leeds gentlemen decided to erect blast furnaces at Ardsley Junction, and their choice of an engineer fell upon Mr. Gjers, who not only undertook to erect the works, but also to carry them on for a certain period after completion. In 1868, the first two blast furnaces of the West Yorkshire Iron Company, as the new concern was named, were blown in successfully, and three more furnaces have since been added. These are the first works of the kind erected in this part of the country. Situated about midway between Leeds and Wakefield, on the line of the Great Northern Railway at its junction with the Bradford branch, and a little to the north of the Methley junction, they have sidings connected with both these railways, and direct communication is thus secured with all the railways in the country. The company are lessees from the late Earl of Cardigan, of a large field of clayband ironstone in the well-known measures of the district, as well as a seam of fine coal adapted for coking and smelting purposes. They are also lessees of, and have opened out, an ironstone mine in Lincolnshire (on the estate of the Earl of Yarborough), where a remarkably pure hydra-ted ironstone is obtained out of the green sandstone measures. This, when smelted in suitable mixture with the local clayband stone, produces a very superior pig iron, which is particularly well suited for the better purposes of the district. The lime used for fluxing is the best Skipton rock.

The remodelling of the old Wingerworth Ironworks in Derbyshire was undertaken by Mr. Gjers in 1868. Here he introduced another novelty, by effecting the perfect utilization of the blast furnace gases with open-topped furnaces. This was really the first succesful attempt to utilise blast furnace gases in that part of the country; and it may be interesting to state that in the carrying out of his own new arrangements Mr. Gjers used a portion of the original tubing made nearly twenty years previously, and abandoned because the object aimed at could not be attained.

Those who are familiar with the life of the famous George Stephenson, will remember that he was for some years the managing and principal partner in the Clay Cross Ironworks, in Derbyshire. These works, we believe, were actually built, and partly, if not wholly, designed by the great engineer; but they were found at a later date to be unsuited to the exigencies of modern science, and in 1869, Mr. Gjers was entrusted with their reconstruction. The latter carried out his work to the entire satisfaction of his employers. The original furnaces were raised from 48 to 60 feet in height, and the diameter of the boshes was increased one foot.

Mr. Gjers was the first Cleveland engineer who obtained a footing in the Lincolnshire iron district. In 1869, he undertook the reconstruction of Frodingham Ironworks, which had been started with two blast furnaces of very limited size and capacity. When it was decided to remove these old furnaces and build an entirely new plant, Mr. Gjers was the engineer selected to execute the work. Four furnaces were put up under his supervision, and it is worthy of note that these furnaces have served as the model for most of the furnaces subsequently built in the neighbourhood of Frodingham. It is probable, also, that it was the skill and engineering capacity displayed by Mr. Gjers that led to the choice by other firms of other Cleveland engineers in the erection of works now going on—the urgent calls of his own business having compelled Mr. Gjers himself to relinquish nearly all other engagements. Within the last two years he has given himself almost entirely up to the management of the Ayresome works, of which more hereafter, although he has very recently been prevailed upon to undertake the designing of an extensive blast furnace plant and Bessemer works in his native country, and in carrying out this commission he will introduce several novelties and improvements that are likely to attract the attention of English engineers.

On the first day of January, 1870, Mr. Gjers commenced the erection of the Ayresome Ironworks, although his professional connection with Messrs. Hopkins, Gilkes, and Company, and Messrs. Lloyd and Company, did not cease until the end of that year. The Ayresome works consist of a plant of four blast furnaces, the two first having been blown in on the 29th March, 1871. They are situated within the borough of Middlesbrough, on 32 acres of land abutting on the river Tees, and having a frontage thereto of 330 yards. These works have received many encomiums from practical engineers, and, taken as a whole, they are probably as great a tribute to the engineering ability of Mr. Gjers as any of the numerous works he had previously designed. The Ayresome works are equal to a production of between 1500 to 1600 tons of pig iron per week.

On the 18th January, 1871, Mr. Gjers was presented with a testimonial by the employers and employees connected with the firm of Hopkins, Gilkes and Company, on the occasion of his finally severing his connection with it. Mr. W. R. I. Hopkins, the senior partner, presided, and in the course of a speech full of complimentary allusions, declared that " Mr. Gjers had gone to them partly an untried and unknown man, but they learned to put so much confidence in him that they placed in his hands the out-door management of the blast furnaces earlier than was the custom. Mr. Gjers had derived from his connection with them, but still more by his own talents, great advantages in his own extended experience as a business man and in the out-door management of blast furnaces, and had now become the senior partner of the firm known as Gjers, Mills, and Company. Mr. Gjers had always been a just manager to the master and workmen, and the result was, that without exemption, they had wished to subscribe to that testimonial."

Having been so actively engaged in professional duties during the greater part of his life, Mr. Gjers has not found time, even if he had the inclination to take any part in municipal or imperial politics. But he has contributed some of the most valuable results of his wide experience to the transactions of the Cleveland Institution of Engineers, and of the Iron and Steel Institute of Great Britain. Before the latter association, in 1871, he read a paper on "The gradual increase in size of the Cleveland blast furnaces," and "A description of the Ayresome Ironworks, Middlesbrough." In the former part of his paper, the author traced the gradual growth in size and capacity of the blast furnaces of Cleveland, from those built by Messrs. Bolckow and Vaughan at their Middlesbrough works in 1851, with a cubical capacity of 4,566 feet, and 42 feet high by 15 feet bosh, to the furnaces erected at Ormesby in 1870, 90 feet high, 50 feet bosh, and 41,149 feet cubical capacity.

XV.—JEREMIAH HEAD.

MOST of the " pioneers " to whom we have, as yet, assigned places in this series, are more or less associated with the development of the pig-iron trade.   It is, however, to another of the staple industries of Cleveland, viz. : that of malleable iron, that the energies of Jeremiah Head, the subject of the present article, have been chiefly directed.   He is the fourth son of the late Jeremiah Head, Esq., J.P., of Ipswich, who was, like his forefathers for several generations, a highly esteemed member of the Society of Friends.

Jeremiah Head, the younger, was born in 1835, and was educated partly at home, partly at private schools in Ipswich, and partly at Tulketh Hall, a Friends' School in Lancashire, which has for some time ceased to exist. Having always evinced a strong inclination towards mechanical pursuits, he was articled in 1851 to the late Robert Stephenson, C.E., M.P., whose engineering works at Newcastle-on-Tyne, have always been reckoned among the first schools of engineering in Europe. After working three and a-half years with the workmen in the shops, he was promoted to the drawing office, where he remained a year and a-half, when his apprenticeship was at an end. Six months previous to this, he had been entrusted with the design, and setting to work, of a large pair of compound condensing engines for Messrs. Henry Pease and Company's Priestgate Mills, Darlington. It was in order to complete this undertaking that he was sent to reside for six weeks in the above-named town. There he became more intimately acquainted with the Pease family, some of whom have been from the first partners in the firm of Robert Stephenson and Company, but without taking any part in the management thereof.

The Priestgate Mills' new engines were the first in this country fitted with a " parabolic governor," the principle of which has since been extensively adopted. The air cataract, a most important adjunct, was Mr. Head's invention ; but being still a pupil he deemed it his duty to offer it to the firm, who patented it in the name of Mr. Weallens, their manager. They subsequently allowed the patent to lapse, but continued to manufacture on the new principle wherever applicable. A modification of the parabolic governor controlled by a liquid cataract, instead of one containing air, has since been found much superior in its action, especially when applied to operate variable expansion gears, and for this Mr. Head still holds a patent.

When the Darlington engines were complete, Mr. Head was entrusted with the design of another pair, into which he introduced some improvements, and these are still at work at Messrs. Annandale and Sons' Paper Mills, Shotley Bridge.

In 1857, the Corporation of Sunderland determined to re-build the bridge which had been erected over the river Wear by Rowland Burdon about a century before, and which had then become unsafe. Robert Stephenson was appointed consulting engineer to this, which proved to be his last great constructive work. He selected Mr. G. A. Phipps of Great George Street, Westminster, to be his acting colleague, and Mr. Head to be resident engineer, in carrying out the undertaking. The construction and erection of the new bridge, of which the span is 240 feet, and the height above high water mark 120 feet, and which involved an outlay of nearly £40,000, occupied two years, and proved a valuable piece of experience. When it was finished Mr. Head had the satisfaction of being presented with a handsome piece of furniture, viz., a what-not, cast from the metal of the original bridge, by Messrs. Hawks, Crawshay, and Sons, the contractors for the iron work. Upon a silver plate were engraved particulars of the circumstances under which it was given. Some time previous to the period of which we speak, the Royal Agricultural Society had offered a prize of £500 for the best steam plough. At two of their annual shows, the prize had been competed for, but none of the machines exhibited were considered sufficiently perfect to deserve it. The late Mr. John Fowler, of the well-known firm of John Fowler and Company, of Leeds, had been giving special attention to the construction of steam cultivating machinery, and was extremely anxious to carry off the Society's award on the third and last occasion when it would be offered. Through his father-in-law, the late Mr. Joseph Pease, of Darlington, Mr. Fowler obtained the interest of Robert Stephenson. That gentleman said that he was too far advanced in life to take a personally active part in new enterprises, but that he would gladly afford any other assistance in his power, for the sake of the partner with whom he had been so long associated. In fulfilment of this promise he introduced Mr. Head, and desired him to direct his energies to the improvement of the steam plough, so as, if possible, to enable Mr. Fowler to acquire the coveted distinction. To Mr. Head the task was highly congenial, and he worked most

assiduously for several months with Mr.
Fowler, against great difficulties and repeated
disappointments. At last they produced at
the classical works of Robert Stephenson and
Company, a steam plough which fulfilled all the
conditions laid down by the Royal Agricultural Society, and which received the prize of
£500 at their Chester Show in 1858. For
about a year steam ploughs continued to be
constructed by Messrs. Robert Stephenson and
Company, under Mr. Head's direction, when it
became evident that some arrangement must
be made for developing the new implement
more rapidly, and manufacturing it on a more
extensive scale, in order to meet the growing
demand. It did not suit Mr. Stephenson to
sacrifice his well established locomotive, and
marine engine business, for one in agricultural
machinery ; he therefore suggested that new
works should be built for the purpose in Newcastle, and offered, in that case, to advance
his old pupil £3,000 to enable him to take up
a partnership in such works, whilst Mr.
Joseph Pease agreed to advance a similar
sum to promote the interests of Mr. Fowler.
Some delay, however, occurred in maturing
these plans, and meanwhile Mr. Stephenson
died, and the whole project fell through. The
development of the steam plough might have
been delayed for several years, but for a new
friend who appeared upon the scene, at this

juncture. The late Mr. W. Hewitson, of Leeds, and offered upon certain terms, to provide the funds necessary for building works on a large scale at Leeds. The offer was too good a one to be declined, and among other arrangements it was agreed that Mr. Head should leave Newcastle for that town, and should be entrusted with the management of the new undertaking, with the option of a partnership after a time. Accordingly, he continued to co-operate with Mr. Fowler for the space of a year, developing the new machine and organising those arrangements for its construction which now occupy so important a place in the industries of the West Riding. "*L'homme propose, mais Dieu dispose.*" So runs the French proverb, and so it came to pass in the present instance. In the summer of 1860, after a year's residence in Leeds, Mr. Head fell ill, and continued unwell for so long a time, that he thought it wise to resign his position at the steam plough works. He had latterly thoroughly over-wrought himself in his efforts to secure the success of the steam plough. For the space of a year he lived quite retired from business, when, feeling much better, and being anxious to gain increased practical experience in the working of the steam plough in the field, he bought one of the most approved construction, and

R

settled down at Swindon, in Wiltshire. That town is the centre of a well-known heavy clay land district, standing in great need of steam cultivation. There he took contracts among the farmers and landed proprietors, for draining and cultivating by steam power, and acted as Messrs. Fowler and Company's representative for the district. Shortly after, he devised and patented a system of lamp signals whereby steam ploughing might be conducted by night as well as by day, a matter of great importance in the autumnal season. He also patented a means of making the "skifes," or castings to which the shares are attached in balance ploughs, adjustable, so as to give them any required amount of "bite" into the ground. Both these patents were afterwards purchased by Mr. Fowler, for use in machines made at his works.

In the spring of 1863 Mr. Head, finding his health completely re-established, determined to give up ploughing and draining by steam, for some occupation which would admit of residence in a more active industrial centre than a small Wiltshire town. He visited the Cleveland district, and came to the conclusion that rolling mills, for the manufacture of boiler and ship plates, at Middlesbrough, would, if carefully constructed and managed, prove a lucrative enterprise. He communicated his views to Mr. Joseph Pease, who,

being then retired from business, referred him
to his son, Mr. J. W. Pease, one of the present
members for South Durham. That gentleman
introduced him to his brother-in-law, Mr.
Theodore Fox, and through Mr. Joseph Dodds,
of Stockton, to Mr. Charles M. Newcomen, of
Kirkleatham. Thus was originated, in 1863,
the present firm of Fox, Head, and Company,
of Middlesbrough.

It was November, 1864, before the works
they decided to construct were complete.
Then began a new series of difficulties.
Wages were extremely high, and trades' unions
were for the moment all-powerful. Their
workmen were so unmanageable, that the
young firm thought it wise to join other
employers in maintaining a union for concerted
action in regard to labour. But a short experience seemed to them to prove that this
policy had the effect rather of aggravating
than of mitigating the evil. During two
years they had lost no less than one-fourth
of their whole time in disputes with their
workmen. So they came to the conclusion
that no solid success could attend their
efforts while they and their employés were
in a constant state of antagonism, however
satisfactory might be their relations towards
competing employers. They drew up their
now well-kown " Co-operative Scheme," con-
stituting their enterprise an industrial partner-

ship. It might have been expected that their workmen would have at once accepted so generous a concession, and would eagerly have become co-operators on so favourable terms. Not so, however. Prominent unionist leaders denounced the new scheme as "a dodge" to allure the men from their union, that they might be the more easily manipulated to their disadvantage by their employers. Articles appeared in journals, supposed to represent the employers' views, which were scarcely less hostile in their tone. A period of great depression in trade had also now supervened, rendering it impossible, during the first two years, to pay any bonus to labour, according to the hopes held out by the scheme. Consequently the workmen were influenced but little by it, and its complete failure was generally predicted. Still, however, Messrs. Fox, Head, and Company persevered, and at the end of the third year, viz.—1869, they had the satisfaction of being able to announce a dividend to their employés of $2\frac{1}{2}$ per cent. upon their yearly earnings. From that time mutual confidence took the place of mutual distrust, between Messrs. Fox, Head, and Company and the majority, including all the best, of their workmen. In 1870, $3\frac{1}{2}$ per cent. was paid; in 1871, 4 per cent.; and in 1872 $3\frac{1}{4}$ per cent., in addition to full district wages. But we have not space to enlarge further on this interesting experiment. The complete history thereof has been published in the shape of reports of the annual meetings of the employers and employed at Newport Rolling Mills. The difficulties attending the development of the system, and the sentiments both of masters and men in regard to it, and to each other, abundantly appear in the speeches therein recorded. The firm are, we believe, always ready to present copies of their reports to those who take an interest in them.

In 1863, when the Newport firm was first constituted, the Cleveland plate trade was in its infancy. At one works alone had this kind of iron hitherto been produced, and there, not of a quality suitable for boiler construction. For such purposes, Staffordshire or South Yorkshire plates were almost invariably used. Ten years later, owing to the efforts of Messrs. Fox, Head, and Company, and some other proprietors of rolling mills, who commenced operations about the same time, a vast improvement in quality had been effected. Boiler work of the most difficult kind, not excepting the manufacture of Galloway tubes, is now habitually executed by firms using none but Cleveland plates.

The Middlesbrough Co-operative Store Company, Limited, which after several years of adversity, has now attained a state of marvellous prosperity, was originated, and has throughout been managed mainly by a few of Messrs. Fox, Head, and Company's employés. It was, we believe, at Mr. Head's suggestion, and by his desire it was started, and its success would perhaps never have been achieved but for the constant sympathy and active assistance of himself and his partners.

Mr. Head's name also appears on the directorate of " The Cleveland Slag Working Company, Limited," the object of which is to utilize slag for bricks, mortar, concrete, etc., according to the patents of Messrs. Wood and Bodmer.

Mr. Head was the founder, in 1865, of the " Cleveland Institution of Engineers." During three years he undertook the onerous duties of honorary secretary, and worked most unremittingly to secure the success which was ultimately attained. In 1871 he was elected president, and still holds that position. Among provincial scientific societies, the Cleveland Institution of Engineers is now generally admitted to occupy a foremost place, and the printed reports of its papers and discussions are highly esteemed, both for their merit as literary works, and for their intrinsic value as scientific records. The original number of members was about 30, now it has reached 320, and includes all those with whom rests the responsibility of practically directing industrial operations in

Cleveland; and many engineers from all parts of the country.

Mr. Head has contributed at various times papers and addresses to the Cleveland Institution, and to other Scientific Societies to which he belongs. The principal of these are as follows, viz. :—

To the Cleveland Institution : — On " A Plan for placing the Cleveland Iron District in better communication with the Durham Coal-field, by means of certain new Railways, and a Bridge over, or a Tunnel under the river Tees;" in 1868. A considerable portion of this scheme was adopted by the North-Eastern Railway Company, in a bill for which they subsequently attempted to obtain Parliamentary sanction, but which was thrown out owing to the opposition of the Corporation of Stockton and other bodies. On "The Economic Construction and Management of Steam Engines and Boilers;" in 1869. (This paper has since been re-printed by desire of the engineer of the Midland Steam Boiler Inspection and Assurance Company, for the special use of his inspectors and others.) Upon " Our Workmen ;" a presidential address delivered in 1871. On "'The Economic Unsoundness of some Trades' Union Doctrines ;" another presidential address delivered in 1872, and again on " Thoughts for the consideration of Engineers and Others," delivered in 1873.

Before the Institution of Mechanical Engineers :—On " The Parabolic Governor ;" in 1871.

Before the Iron and Steel Institute: —On " The Efficiency and Durability of Plain Cylindrical Boilers ;" in 1870. On " Fox, Head and Company's Patent Economical Puddling Furnaces ;" in 1871. On "The Linthorpe Boiler Explosion;" in 1873. On " An Improved Reversing Gear for Rolling Mills ;" in 1873.

Before the National Association for the promotion of Social Science :—On " Retail Traders and Co-operative Stores ;" in 1872.

· Before the Bristol and Clifton Debating Society :—On " The Newport Industrial Partnership, etc. ;" in 1873.

Before the British Association for the Advancement of Science, Section G, on " A Higher Education for Engineers," read at their meeting at Belfast, in 1874.

Mr. Head is a most regular attender at the meetings of the various scientific societies with which he is connected, and has always taken an active part in their discussions. On the visit to Middlesbrough, in 1871, of the Institution of Mechanical Engineers, he and Mr. Gilbert Gilkes acted as local secretaries, and made the various and somewhat complex arrangements which were necessary to secure the success of that meeting. He has since been elected to a seat upon the Council.

JEREMIAH HEAD. 281

Middlesbrough is the first town in England
which applied for a school board under the
Elementary Education Act, and Mr. Head
was among the nine gentlemen elected to
seats at the first board.   He has always shown
the greatest interest in all endeavours to
diffuse knowledge, whether of an elementary
or technical character.   He has not hitherto
taken part in municipal affairs, probably for
want of time.   But in general politics he has
given abundant proof that he is a decided and
even enthusiastic Liberal, endorsing the policy
of the late Government, and exerting all his
personal influence in their support.

XVI.—EDWARD WILLIAMS.

" The true epic of our time," says Carlyle,
" is not arms and the man, but tools and the
man—an infinitely wider kind of epic."
When he speaks of tools, the Chelsea philosopher refers, of course, to every possible
kind of mechanical appliance, calculated to
abrogate manual labour, and further the interests of the industrial arts. In this sphere
of thought and action, Mr. Edward Williams
has long laboured. He possesses, perhaps, a
wider acquaintance with the varying processes
and apparatus used in connection with the
iron trade of this and other countries than
many men who have theorised on the subject
for a lifetime, and have come at last to be
regarded and quoted as authorities of unimpeachable exactitude and soundness. In all
essential points, Mr. Williams may be spoken
of as a practical man. He has studied for
himself, under every condition, the *rationale*
of the industries in which he is employed.
Accepting the *ipse dixit* of no one, he has

earned the reputation of being an original thinker and worker, and there are those who contemn his disregard of the old established rules and canons, as savouring too much of the mental idiosyncracy which so peculiarly characterised Thomas called Didymus. But it is to this faculty of personal investigation and research more than any other that the pre-eminent industrial position now held by the North of England is mainly due. Had the pioneers of the Cleveland Iron Trade been content to follow the beaten path, so long traversed by the older iron-producing districts, turning neither to the right nor to the left, many, if not most, of the results that have been recorded in these articles would never have been attained. The historian's duty would have been more simple; but it would have been less pleasant and less useful. A dead level of uniformity would have characterised that which is now distinguished for diversity, and presents abundant scope for a conflict of opinion. When many different roads are followed towards the same goal, the shortest and easiest is more likely to become known, and in the long run, adopted by those who had previously wandered in a devious course. So it is with the iron trade. Out of the many and somewhat confused formulæ that are now adopted, order and certitude will, no doubt, ultimately be evolved. It is in the furtherance of this great end that such men as Mr. Williams are employed; and it is now impossible to calculate the far-reaching advantages which are reflected by their labours on the cause of progress and civilisation. For it is well to remember that, although it is strictly a scientific pursuit, metallurgy cannot yet claim a place among the exact sciences. There is much yet to be learned. There are many possible economies still unfulfilled. The splendid results achieved during the last ten or twenty years supply ample proof of the fact that perfection is a long way ahead—that we are only nearing the beginning of the end.

Viewed in the light of the foregoing remarks the career of Mr. Edward Williams is one well worth study. He was born in Merthyr Tydvil—the Dudley of Staffordshire, the Middlesbrough of Cleveland, the Coatbridge of Scotland. From his youth up he was among ironworks and ironworkers. His father was a schoolmaster. The Academy of Taliesin Williams was esteemed one of the best in South Wales. It was the nursery of many minds that have stamped with the sign manual of their genius the graduated progress of our staple industry. The master of the academy was a man of more than average attainments.

> " He was kind, or if severe in aught,
> The love he bore to learning was in fault."

The most that could be said of Goldsmith's
" Village Schoolmaster" was, that

" Lands he could measure, terms and tides presage;"

but Taliesin Williams could do more than
,that. In a district where the amenities of
literature were little known, he cultivated the
muses, not unsuccessfully. One of his peices
—an ode to Cardiff Castle, written after the
style of Scott's " Lady of the Lake"—is
familiarly known to this day. The Williams
family thus owned a highly respectable position in Merthyr Tydvil—a position certifi-
cated by the tradition that they could trace
their descent collaterally to Oliver Cromwell.

Edward Williams received as good an education as it was within the far from stinted
limits of his father's means to bestow. He
then entered the office of the Dowlais Ironworks—the largest establishment of its kind in
the world. Here his experience was a re-
versal of the rule that " a prophet hath not
honour in his own country." His promotion
was rapid and deserved. The then mill manager at Dowlais took a special interest in his
training; and through him Mr. Williams
acquired a thorough knowledge, both theoretical and practical, of the properties of iron
and its manipulation. It is quite a prevalent
belief that he was, like the late late Mr. John
Vaughan, brought up as an ironworker, but
we have reason to know that this is quite an
error. He never was directly employed in

the works, otherwise than as far as was necessary to enable him to understand the
rationale of iron manufacture. But his experience, such as it was, must have been of the
most valuable character. At the Dowlais works
every branch of the iron trade is carried on
to the largest extent. There are no fewer
than seventeen blast furnaces—more than
double the number in operation at the largest
works on Teesside—while the number of
puddling furnaces is upwards of 160 ! Speaking of these works, Mr. Ferdinand Kohn, C.E.,
author of a standard work on the manufacture
of iron and steel, says " Dowlais ! the name of
no other place in Britain so strongly and fully
expresses the tremendous power of British
iron and British coal—a power which has made
our country the first among the nations of the
earth. France has its Creusot, with its fourteen blast furnaces, and giving employment
to 10,000 men ; Belgium has its Seraing, with
five furnaces and extensive workshops, never
again to be what they once were, when John
Cockerill, an Englishman too, and having the
King of Holland for his partner, was living.
We will not dispute the greatness of Essen,
nor need we refer to the comparatively insignificant centres of the iron industry of America—Phœnixville and Johnstown. But where
France, and Belgium, and Prussia may have
large individual works, Dowlais, with its

seventeen blast furnaces, and its nine thousand
workpeople, nevertheless makes but one-thir-
tieth of all our iron, and raises less than the
one-hundredth part of all our coal." It may
be remarked here that the establishment over
which Mr. Williams now presides is modelled
on the works of Dowlais. Both have very
large ironworks for the manufacture of both
crude and finished iron ; both have large ironstone and coal royalties, from which they
raise all their own minerals ; both carry on
the manufacture of Bessemer steel to a large
extent ; and both have all the necessary works
and appliances for the manufacture of such
subsidiary products as fire bricks, rolling
stock and general machinery. There are
many minor and collateral points of resem-
blance upon which more may be said hereafter.
Meanwhile, it must be apparent that Mr Williams had the advantage of being trained in a
good school—the best, probably, that this or
any other country contains, and one, more-
over, that has made its name famous all the
world over. After having been employed at
their works for a number of years, he was
sent to London as the Metropolitan agent of
the Dowlais Company—a position involving
much care, judgment, and responsibility. It
was here and in this capacity that he was
employed when the works and business of
Bolckow and Vaughan were transferred to a

limited liability company. The late Mr. John Vaughan, who had previously undertaken the practical management of the concern, was, of course, indisposed to do so any longer; and he was requested by the directors to recommend a suitable successor. Numerous applications from some of the best men in the country were sent in; but the choice of the directors was finally limited to two gentlemen. One of these was Mr. Evans, another Welshman, now the manager of the celebrated Bowling ironworks, Bradford; the other was Mr. Edward Williams. It is a somewhat noteworthy coincidence that both had been more or less intimately connected with Dowlais Works from their earliest years—the father of Mr. Evans having long been manager of Dowlais. Bolckow, Vaughan, and Company, (Limited) was formed in 1864. The capital of the company was fixed at £2,500,000, and £1,000,000, was paid for the purchase of the properties and stock. Messrs. Bolckow and Vaughan took 8,000 shares, paying £50 per share, and agreed that no dividend should be paid upon these 8,000 shares until an average dividend equal to ten per cent. per annum should have been paid for five years to the other shareholders. Since then the nominal capital of the company has been increased to £3,410,000. Under Mr. Williams' management, the company was enjoyed a prosperity

and attained a stability almost without parallel in the annals of limited liability. It is
now probably the largest concern of its kind
in the world. It has even taken precedence
of the great Dowlais works, and of the scarcely less famous Gartsherrie works in Scotland,
each of which employ about 9,000 hands, as
compared with nearly 12,000 employed by
Bolckow, Vaughan, and Company. In addition to the blast furnaces at Middlesbrough,
Eston, and Witton Park, the rolling mills at
the former and the latter places, and the
great mines at Eston and Skelton, it holds,
with perhaps only two or at the most three
exceptions, the largest coal royalties in the
North of England, and carries on large steel
works in Manchester. Upwards of £16,000
are paid weekly in wages and salaries. The
company raise about 1,500,000 tons of coal
per annum ; and from their Eston mines alone
they are now producing between 700,000 and
800,000 tons of ore. Of the 250,000 tons of
pig iron which they annually produce, the
company convert nearly 100,000 into rails,
plates, bars, and other descriptions of manufactured iron. They have within the last few
years acquired large royalties in Spain, and
from their mines at Bilbao they raise large
quantities of hematite, for the conveyance of
which to their Middlesbrough works they employ a fleet of steamers of their own. Like
s

the Dowlais works, Messrs. Bolckow and Vaughan's establishment has every facility for the production of general machinery, castings, firebricks, and rolling stock; and the number of wagons which they own and employ in connection with their numerous works and collieries is something fabulous—larger than that of many a respectable railway company. The same remark applies to their locomotive engines, which are also, for the most part, manufactured at their own works, to their private railway lines, connecting their different collieries with each other and with their works, and to the value of their goods and mineral traffic. It may truly be said of Bolckow, Vaughan, and Company's works, as we have seen it said of Dowlais, that " so long as metallurgical industry holds its accustomed footing in the affairs of the kingdom, so long will these works be famous as a monument of the energy and genius of their founders and of the proudest age of British industrial and commercial power."

If these, then, are the works over which he acts as the presiding genius, what must be the nature and extent of the duties that Mr. Williams is called upon to discharge? A bare contemplation of them would almost be sufficient to turn the brain of an ordinary mortal. And yet every movement of this huge industrial machine is guided by his hand. Down to the merest trifle, he regulates and governs the affairs of the firm. He shirks no duty or responsibility, by vicarious substitution. Every appointment of any consequence is made by himself after the most careful and patient inquiry. He is the fountain of authority in the making of all important contracts, in the introduction of new machinery and processes, and in the carrying out of the multiform arrangements that require settlement from day to day. It is necessary, above all things, that the responsible manager of such a large concern should receive emoluments commensurate with his position. The universal verdict is that he is quite worthy of his position; and both directors and shareholders have confidence that so long as he is at the helm of affairs, all will go well.

Although the North of England iron trade was undoubtedly established before Mr. Williams came to Middlesbrough, he is not without claims to a place among its conscript fathers. Even so far back as 1864 Cleveland was in a comparatively embryo state. "Enterprises of great pith and moment" were in process of being evolved, but they wanted accessory aids that were yet undeveloped. Mr. Williams, from the first day that he entered the district, threw himself heart and soul into the work of promoting reforms and improvements calculated to benefit the trade as a whole. He was president of the North of England Ironmasters' Association in 1868, when the Iron and Steel Institute of Great Britain was founded, and he was chairman of the meeting held in the Newcastle Assembly Rooms, on the 28th September of that year, at which the idea of projecting such an institute was first mooted. It may be remembered that the institute owed its origin to a suggestion made by Mr. John Jones, secretary to the North of England Ironmasters' Association, in a paper which he read on " The position of the iron trade in relation to technical education," and that suggestion was subsequently formulated in a motion proposed by Mr. Isaac Lowthian Bell, to the effect " that this meeting approves of the proposition contained in the paper read by Mr. Jones, relative to the establishment of an Iron and Steel Institute, and requests that a Provisional Committee be nominated, consisting of the following gentlemen, with power to add to their number, viz :—Mr. Edward Williams, Middlesbrough ; Mr. Isaac L. Bell and Mr. James Morrison, Newcastle ; Mr. David Dale, Darlington ; Mr. J. J. Smith, Barrow ; Mr. W. Fletcher, Workington ; Mr. Pattison, Warrington ; Mr. G. J. Barker, Chillington ; Mr. Walter Williams, Tipton ; Mr. Wm. Matthews, Dudley ; Mr. W. S. Roden, Stoke ; Mr. Robert

Heath, Stoke; Mr. W. Menelaws, Dowlais; Mr. A. Brogden, London; Mr. R. Fothergill; Mr. F. Kitson, Leeds; Sir J. G. W. Alleyne, Bart., Butterly; Sir John Brown, Sheffield; Mr. Neilson, Glasgow; Mr. Samuelson, Banbury; and Mr. John Jones, Middlesbrough." It will thus be observed that although the Iron and Steel Institute owes its origin to Cleveland, there are only two gentlemen on the committee under whom it has been enabled to attain such high measure of success who belonged directly to Middlesbrough. From time to time Mr. Williams has contributed his valuable experience to the transactions of the Institute; and at the first provincial meeting held in Middlesbrough in 1869, he read a paper on the manufacture of rails, which was spoken of very highly by those who afterwards discussed its merits and conclusions. The subject of rail manufacture is one to which Mr. Williams has devoted a great deal of attention, and it may be remarked in this connection that he has not unfrequently been consulted as to its *rationale.* The best tribute that can be paid to the soundness and merit of a practical man is the respect and deference of other practical men. It has been Mr. Williams' destiny to take up a position in which his statements are regarded by his *collaborateurs* as coming from an authority. There is no sciolism about his researches and opinions. He goes straight to the root of the matter, and is always able to give a reason for the faith that is in him. In regard to blast furnace practice, Mr. Williams has expressed himself in favour of high furnaces; and, unlike some other authorities on the subject, he believes that the increase of economy in the mordern furnace is due more to height than to capacity. Discrediting some of the prevailing ideas as to the temperature of the blast, he concludes that less depends upon that element than upon the chemical composition of the gases. " If," he says, "the gas contains a large quantity of carbonic acid, we may be sure the furnace is working with a small amount of coke; but if, on the other hand, the gas contains a large amount of carbonic oxide, then we may conclude that the coke is being used wastefully." " The subject of mechanical puddling has received from Mr. Williams a great deal of attention. He has all along been a member of the Puddling Committee of the Iron and Steel Institute, and in that capacity he has conducted and witnessed many experiments of a valuable kind. It was under the auspices of this committee that a Commission of practical ironmasters visited Cincinatti, U.S., to report upon the Danks's puddling machine, which is now being largely introduced into the Cleveland district; and it was on the suggestion and advice of Mr. Williams that this was done. To him, therefore, belongs the honour, such as it is, of having secured a fair and dispassionate trial for the Danks's rotary puddler, and of taking the necessary steps to bring its merits prominently before the iron-masters of the country. Previous, however, to the invention of the Danks machine, Mr. Menelaus, manager of the Dowlais works, had long sought to develop and bring to a successful issue the idea of mechanical puddling. In this effort he was aided more or less directly by his friend, Mr. Williams, who took quite a feverish interest in the subject. Mr. Menelaus did not succeed in solving the problem of successful mechanical puddling, principally from the absence of a suitable fettling; but at the Middlesbrough works of Messrs. Bolckow and Vaughan, a machine constructed on Mr. Menelaus's principle has been under trial for a considerable time, and Mr. Williams is hopeful of ultimately overcoming the difficulties in the way of effective fettling.

For the last six or eight years the subject of these remarks has hammered away at the door of the North-Eastern Board until he has obtained from that company a meed of consideration towards Middlesbrough that would probably never have been vouchsafed but for his assiduity. One of first movements he took up was that for the construction of new docks. Middlesbrough was wretchedly off for dock accommodation, the entrance of the existing docks being both narrow and shallow, while there were no quay walls, crane facilities, or other necessary provision for shippers at all commensurate with the importance of the port. Chiefly, we believe, at Mr. Williams's instigation, a public meeting of the inhabitants of Middlesbrough was held in the Town Hall on the 3rd day of June, 1868, to take the subject of better and increased dock accommodation into consideration. At that meeting Mr. Williams, who was one of the chief spokesmen, proposed a motion to the effect that the trade and prosperity of the town and district were seriously affected in consequence of inadequate dock accommodation, and he mentioned, as an illustration of the fact, that during the previous year Messrs. Bolckow and Vaughan had sent 67,000 tons of their produce to neighbouring ports that should have been shipped at Middlesbrough. A deputation, of which Mr. Williams was a member, was appointed to wait on the North Eastern Board; and the result of their representations and labours is apparent in the largely extended and improved docks which Middlesbrough now possesses at a cost to the railway company of over £100,000.

There are not a few other phases, all more

or less interesting, of Mr. Williams' career
that might be appropriately referred to, but
they are for the most part of such recent
origin and occurrence that the briefest possible
allusion must suffice. The Freighters Association recently formed in Middlesbrough to
protect the iron trade from the imposition of
excessive dues by the railway company chiefly
owes its origin to him. He is an active
member of the Middlesbrough Chamber of
Commerce, of the Middlesbrough Town Council, and of other local institutions. In religion, Mr. Williams is said to be a member
of the Church of England; in politics, he is a
thorougly sound Liberal; and in private and
social life, he is one of the most genial and
pleasant of men, leaving behind him, whether
at home or abroad, a human and refreshing
memory.

XVII.—JAMES MORRISON.

SOME men, it is said, are born great; some achieve greatness, while some again have greatness thrust upon them. Mr. James Morrison belongs neither to the first nor to the third of these three divisions; but so far as any claim he has established to greatness is concerned, he may undoubtedly be included in the second. And his title to distinction is higher than that of many a man who has made a much greater noise in the world. If the somewhat trite aphorism that the man is entitled to honour and does a good work who makes two blades of grass grow where only one grew before, then is James Morrison worthy to stand on the highest rung of the ladder of fame. In a quiet and unobtrusive, but none the less effectual way, he has initiated many economical reforms that have had more than merely local and tentative advantages; and no man has been more intimately connected during the last forty years with the iron trade of the North of England.

While his career has been chequered and eventful, even to the borders of romance, it has also been successful beyond those of his contemporaries, illustrating with vivid force the story of the old man, his son, and the bundle of sticks.

James Morrison, the founder of the Ferry-hill Ironworks, was born in the year 1806, in Glamorganshire, South Wales, so that he is now in the sixty-seventh year of his age. His father was in comparatively humble circumstances, and belonged,· as well as his mother, to Northumberland, where they had spent their earlier years. James was of a bold, adventrous disposition. He was placed in an office for some time, but he did not care much for the routine of office work, and when only nineteen years of age, despite the wishes and entreaties of his friends to the contrary, he went to South America in connection with the Poliso Mining Company, which company failed before he reached the mines, and he was thrown on his own resources. Little is known of his career, during the next few years. In South America, then much more even than now, a lawless and unsettled country, he was compelled to "rough it" as best he could, until a convenient opportunity was afforded him for returning to England.

About the year 1830 we find Mr. Morrison, then in his twenty-second year, becoming

connected with the iron and coal trades of
Monmouthshire. The prospects opened up
by this sphere of operations did not, however,
answer his expectations, although, both from
his earlier associations, which were largely
mixed up with the staple industry of South
Wales, and from his short experience after his
return from America, he had gained a considerable insight into the *rationale* of the trade
in which he was afterwards to take such a
leading part. About the year 1836 he quitted
Wales, and found his way to the North of
England. At that time the Ridsdale Ironworks had just been completed. They were
erected by some gentlemen connected with,
or at one time forming part of, the Derwent
Iron Company. There were then only two
works of the kind in operation throughout
the whole of the North of England. These
were the Lemington Ironworks, which were
erected about the year 1800, for the purpose
of smelting stone got from the coal measures
in the neighbourhood of Walbottle, Elswick,
and other places on or adjoining the river
Tyne; and the Birtley Ironworks, consisting
of three furnaces, which were erected about
the year 1828, for the smelting of ironstone
found in the coal measures of Ouston, Birtley,
and the immediate district. The Ridsdale
Ironworks, situated on the north Tyne, were
intended for the clay ironstone obtained in

the carboniferous limestone measures of the neighbourhood. Ascertaining that the new works required a manager, Mr. Morrison made application for and received the appointment. He only continued here, however, for a short time. The works were carried on under many disadvantages. Situated in a very isolated position, the transit of material had to be effected by the use of carts, so that they were debarred from access to other and cheaper ores than those found in the immediate neighbourhood. Worse than all, the local ironstone and coal were obtained in scanty and unreliable supplies, at a heavy cost for mining, while the amount paid for the removal of manufactured produce involved another considerable sacrifice. In the face of all these difficulties, the works had to be abandoned after a few years; and although they were subsequently sold to and carried on by Messrs. Foster and Company, they could not, under the more economical conditions of working that were coming into vogue in other parts of the North, be carried on to advantage. We need not add that they now exist only as a memory of the past.

On the establishment of the Consett Iron Works, in 1840, Mr. Morrison was elected to fill a responsible position in connection with their management. This was a much more extensive and important venture than the

Ridsdale Works. The Consett Iron Company originally commenced operations with seven blast furnaces, intended for the smelting of ironstone from the local coal measures. This source of supply proving inefficient, the carboniferous limestone measures of the Wear and Tyne had to be put under requisition, and quantities were occasionally obtained from the Whitby district. At the best, however, the supply of ore was always fragmentary and precarious, until the Cleveland ironstone began to be used in the year 1851, since which time the Consett Iron Works—now grown to the huge proportions of a second Dowlais—have used the oolitic ores almost exclusively.

For reasons with which we are unacquainted, but most probably because he wanted still further to mature his experience by seeing for himself the blast furnace practice of of the Continent, Mr. Morrison in 1845 went over to France, and became connected as manager and principal proprietor of the Guines and Marquise Works—the former about six miles south of Calais, and the latter nearly the same distance from Boulogne. Both works were of considerable size. They comprised both blast furnaces and rolling mills, the two works being about two miles apart. This and other drawbacks in regard to the economical supply of minerals, and adequate facilities of transport, led to the abandonment of the works at Guines. While they were carried on, however, they achieved a high reputation, second only in France to that of M. Schneider's great Creuzot works. Mr. Morrison remained at Guines until after the French Revolution of 1848, when he became connected with the Rosieres Works, also in France, under somewhat singular circumstances. It is scarcely necessary to say that the effect of the Revolution was to paralyse trade, at least temporarily, in all its ramifications. The ducal proprietor of Rosieres having retired, his bankers made Mr. Morrison an offer to wind up the concern, and carry on the works until certain contracts were completed. This Mr. Morrison-undertook to do at a fixed contract price. Under the circumstances, he was almost able to dictate his own terms, and, of course, he made a handsome profit out of the transaction.

In March, 1851, Mr. Morrison again crossed the Channel, and settled down in Newcastle, where, it may be added, he has since continued to reside. And now we approach what is undoubtedly the most interesting epoch in his career. While in France, in connection with a French engineer, he had invented an ingenious process for purifying small coals by washing out the impurities with which they are mixed. His intention was to develop this process in the North of England, where nothing of the kind had previously been successfully attempted. It was then the custom at all the north-country collieries to burn at the pit mouth the immense accumulations of small coal or "duff," which was obtained as the residue of the screening process. The waste of fuel thus permitted was enormous. Coal was then comparatively a drug in the market. Only the finer qualities were used for manufacturing and domestic purposes. Many thousands of tons that would now command 6s to 10s per ton, and even more, were deliberately burned to waste; and coalowners were glad to allow the "duff" or small coal to be taken away free of cost. Nay more, they endeavoured in many cases to make contracts with ironmasters and others to deliver the coal for 1s 6d to 2s per ton, or a fraction over the cost of carriage. In these circumstances Mr. Morrison had no difficulty in making arrangements for the supply of an almost unlimited quantity of "duff," and we have been informed that the whole of the despised and rejected material from Earl Durham's collieries was placed at his disposal on merely nominal terms. Having made these advantageous arrangements, he subjected the "duff" to his new washing process, which consisted in raising the coals by means of buckets attached to endless chains, and then precipitating them into a basket, where an agitator forced through the coal a stream of water sufficient to precipitate them again (by reason of their lightness and their near approach to the same specific gravity as water), over the spout into a wagon, the pyrites and heavier articles sinking to the bottom, and being let off by a valve constructed for the purpose. The cost of washing a ton of coals in this way was only about 1½d, and Mr. Nicholas Wood estimated that the percentage of loss, depending on their degree of purity and on their size, was in duff of the Hutton Seam about 22 per cent.; in pea small and duff, about 18; and in rough small, about 14 per cent. After the small coal had thus been purified, it was admirably adapted for the manufacture of coke, yielding from 50 to 58 per cent. of that material. To this purpose it was converted by Mr. Morrison, who established coke manufactories on a large scale, and made extensive contracts with ironmasters for the supply of that necessary component in blast furnace practice. The result was a grand success. Able to manufacture coke at from 4s 6d to 5s 6d per ton, Mr. Morrison made large contracts to supply it to ironmasters for more than double that amount. For coke, even when it was the greatest drug and most unmarketable, was seldom sold at less than 7s 6d per ton; and

T

at the present time, as ironmasters know to
their cost, it cannot be had under 42s to 45s
per ton. For several years after he had
initiated this lucrative process, Mr. Morrison
found himself rapidly amassing wealth. He
established works at Coxhoe, Thornley, Wigan,
in Lancashire, and Staveley, in Derbyshire.
He became probably the largest coke manufacturer in the world. None could compete
with him, far less undersell him; so that he
was almost without a rival. This was probably the greatest achievement of his life; it
was at any rate the stepping stone of the
events that are to follow.

In 1859 Mr. Morrison commenced the
Ferryhill Ironworks, erecting three blast
furnaces, each 55 feet in height. Five years
later he amalgamated his interest in these
and other works in the county of Durham
with the owners of the Rosedale estate. Since
then the amalgamated concerns have been
carried on under the style of the Rosedale and
Ferryhill Iron Company (Limited).

Many of our readers will be aware that Mr.
Morrison's partners are Mr. George Leeman,
member for York city, and chairman of the
North-Eastern Railway Company, and Alex-
ander Clunes Sheriff, M.P. for Worcester, and
formerly general manager of that company.
About the year 1860 these gentlemen acquired
the Rosedale estate, and large adjoining

royalties of ironstone. It was a magnificent speculation, and in view of the results that followed, it seems wonderful that it was not developed at an earlier period. Iron is known to have been made in this district six hundred years ago ; but it was not till 1834, in modern times, that the peculiar properties of the minerals of Rosedale Abbey received attention, nor was it until Messrs. Leeman and Sheriff acquired their royalties that it was worked on a scale of any importance. These gentlemen came upon an immense basin or quarry of magnetic ironstone, about 120 feet in thickness, and known to all the metallurgists and mineralogists of the North as Rosedale magnetic ore. Among its many other singular properties this stone, although attracted by the magnet, before calcining, will only, with some very rare exceptions, attract iron itself. It contains from 48 to 50 per cent. of metallic iron, whereas the best part of the main seam of the Cleveland ironstone proper contains no more than 33 per cent. The Rosedale ore is thus much more valuable than that of the Cleveland district proper. The magnetic. ironstone of Rosedale Abbey has been a fertile subject of discussion among scientific men during the last twenty years. It has been treated on by the late Mr. Nicholas Wood, by Mr. J. Bewick, and by Mr. John Marley, of Darlington ; and it is the subject of an interesting discussion in Spon's "Dictionary of Engineering," published in 1869. It appears so suddenly and is all at once developed to such an immense thickness that it is unlike anything else of the same kind that has ever been found in the North of England. Opinions differ very materially as to its origin. Mr. Bewick propounded the theory that it was of volcanic origin, but Mr. Isaac Lowthian Bell and other able mineralogists have disputed this idea. In any case, there the wonderful formation is; and we have mainly to deal with the fact that it has been a source of immense profit to the proprietors. From the time that the present proprietors took possession in July, 1864, until midsummer of 1870, they had landed about 500,000 tons of the magnetic ore of Rosedale West; and in the previous three and a-quarter years, from April 1861, about 250,000 tons had been raised. Since, 1870, however, mining operations have been greately extended. New drifts have been opened on the East Rosedale estate, and at the present time the output of ore averages from 2,500 to 3,000 tons per day.

From the mines at Rosedale to the furnaces at Ferryhill is an easy and natural transition, although much more natural than easy, the stone having to be carried by a route so circuitous as to remind one almost irresist-

ably of poor Dick Swiveller's ill-fated attempt
to get across the street. There are now eight
furnaces erected at Ferryhill, and other two
are in course of being built. And such
furnaces! Two of them are 80 feet in height,
and 18 feet bosh; other four are 81 feet
high, and 21 feet bosh; while the remaining
two are 103 feet in height, and 31 feet bosh.
The two latter are the largest furnaces in the
world. Even their great height is, however,
to be eclipsed by that of two new furnaces,
which will tower to an altitude of 105 feet!
A few parenthetical comments on this subject
of blast furnace dimensions may both interest
and instruct the reader.

The first blast furnace built in Cleveland,
was like the Staffordshire and Scotch furnaces,
carried to the height of only 42 feet. Up to
the year 1858 there was a gradual increase
in size, the highest furnace then built being
56 feet in height, by 16 feet 4 inches bosh.
In 1864 Mr. Thomas Vaughan built a furnace
81 feet in height and 19 feet bosh. By this
time the advantages of an increased height
in the blast furnace were scientifically understood. It was found at first that the larger
furnaces yielded better results than the
smaller ones; but the precise character of
these advantages was rather guessed at than
strictly formulated. Now it is acknowledged
on all hands that it means an economy of fuel

varying from 6 to 10 cwts. of coke, in addition
to increasing the production proportionately
to the size of the furnace, and improving the
quality of the iron, which is now more highly
carbonized and more uniformly soft throughout than it formerly was. The discovery of
these advantages led to a revolution in blast
furnace practice that has had no parallel since
the time when Neilson substituted hot for
cold blast about 1830. Since 1858, nearly
every original furnace built in the Cleveland
district has been demolished, and furnaces of
nearly double their size, and more than double
their capacity, have been erected in their
stead. It is difficult to comprehend all that
this revolution involved. It represented in
the first place an enormous loss in the substitution of new for old plant; it led also to
the prevalence of incertitude and groping as
to possible results which has not yet been
completely overcome. There is still a great
conflict of opinion as to the effects of high
blast furnaces, and the exact height to which
they can advantageously be carried. Much
depends upon the kind and quality of the
burden used in the furnace. Thus, the Durham coal makes exceedingly hard coke, which
is capable of bearing a great burden in the
blast furnace; whereas, in Scotland, where
splint coal is used in its raw state, all attempts
hitherto made to increase the height of the

blast furnace have resulted in failure ; exception being made, of course, in favour of Ferrie's self-coking furnace, where the raw coal becomes coked in passing down a series of chambers at the top of the furnace, before reaching the body, where the real work of smelting is done. Mr. Morrison, at the Ferryhill Works, has carried the argument in favour of high blast furnaces to its extremest limits. His 103 feet furnaces are eight feet higher than the next largest furnace in Cleveland, and when we say Cleveland we mean, of course, the whole world, for nowhere else have blast furnaces been carried to anything like the same height. The results obtained in these monster furnaces have apparently convinced Mr. Morrison that he has not yet reached the limit of height to which furnaces may be built with advantage, seeing that he is now building other two which are to be carried to an altitude of 105 feet. Ironmasters will watch these furnaces with eager interest, many of them being incredulous of the wisdom which has actuated their construction. The cubical capacity of the new furnaces will be close on 50,000 feet ; that of the first furnace built at Middlesbrough by Messrs. Bolckow and Vaughan was only 4,566 feet. Extremes meet here with a vengeance ! But, after all, the increase of height and capacity in the blast furnaces of Cleveland only symbolises and illustrates the advances made by the district in every phase of material progress within the period under record.

The weekly production of the eight furnaces now blowing at Ferryhill is about 3,500 tons. When the two new furnaces are blown, the weekly make of pig iron will be little short of 5,000 tons per week, or a larger make than any other establishment in the North of England. The works have everything within themselves. They have lately drawn a large portion of their supplies of coke and coal from Thrislington and Coxhoe Collieries, both of which are the property of the company. Limestone is quarried on the company's "liberty" about a couple of miles distant from the works. Loam, sand, and fire clay are also found in abundance on the company's ground, and within easy access of the works.

But the mechanical appliances of Ferryhill are scarcely less wonderful than the furnaces. The largest blowing cylinder measures 10ft. 10in. by 10ft. 6in., and we are not surprised to learn that it is one of the largest in the world. Altogether the apparatus that actuate these immense works are on a scale worthy of them ; and it may be said of the concern as a whole that it is a fitting monument to the enterprise of its proprietor.

Besides his interest in the Rosedale and Ferryhill Iron Company, Mr. Morrison is the

owner of collieries in Northumberland and
works at Staveley in Derbyshire. He is a
partner in the Manvers Main (South Yorkshire) and the Renishaw (Derbyshire) Ironworks; and in other ventures of a smaller and
less prominent kind he is more or less
interested.

For a number of years Mr. Morrison has
been a member of the Newcastle Town Council,
and has taken an active part in its deliberations. He has filled the civic chair for two
successive years. In politics Mr. Morrison is
a Radical. This fact will scarcely be credited,
perhaps, by those who heard or read a speech
which he delivered more than four years ago,
at a meeting of the North of England Ironmasters' Association, held in Newcastle. He
was reported to have said that technical education was not for the working classes, that
there must be " hewers of wood and drawers
of water," and that he liked to see the shoe-
maker sticking to his last, and the blacksmith
attending to his forge, adding an expression
which created some scandal at the time. For
this speech Mr. Morrison was severely taken
to task by several papers of that day;
but as he afterwards explained it away, we
may charitably conclude that it was only
an after dinner flourish, and that he holds
opinions more in harmony with the genius
and instincts of advanced Liberalism. In

U

political movements, as such, Mr. Morrison has, however, taken little part. Nor has he been prominently identified with any of our learned and scientific societies, although his name will be found on the rolls of the Iron and Steel Institute, of the North of England Institute of Mining and Mechanical Engineers, and of other societies of a kindred character.

In 1846, Mr. Morrison was married to Miss Taylor, a daughter of the late Mr. Thomas Taylor, of Earsdon. He has a family of three sons and two daughters.

www.ingramcontent.com/pod-product-compliance
Lightning Source LLC
Chambersburg PA
CBHW021215270326
41929CB00010B/1142